Conspiracy
Historical Perspectives

CONSPIRACY: HISTORICAL PERSPECTIVES

Advisory Editors
Phyllis Orlikoff Flug
Michael J. Miller

Advisory Board
George J. Alexander
O. John Rogge

LEGAL CONCEPTS
OF CONSPIRACY

A Law Review Trilogy
1922-1970

ARNO PRESS
A New York Times Company
New York   1972

Reprint Edition 1972 by Arno Press Inc.

"Criminal Conspiracy" (Reprinted from Harvard
Law Review, Vol. XXXV) was reprinted from a
copy in The Princeton University Library

"The Conspiracy Dilemma" (Reprinted from Harvard
Law Review, Vol. 62)
Copyright © 1948 by The Harvard Law Review
Association
Reprinted by permission of The Harvard Law Review
Association

"The Logic of Conspiracy" (Reprinted from
Wisconsin Law Review, Vol. 1970)
Copyright © 1970 by the University of Wisconsin
Reprinted by permission of Wisconsin Law Review

Conspiracy: Historical Perspectives
ISBN for complete set: 0-405-04150-0
See last pages of this volume for titles.

Manufactured in the United States of America

Publisher's Note: The selections in this
compilation were reprinted from the best
available copies.

Library of Congress Cataloging in Publication Data
Main entry under title:

Legal concepts of conspiracy.

   (Conspiracy: historical perspectives)
   CONTENTS: Criminal conspiracy, by F. B. Sayre.
(Reprinted from Harvard law review, v. XXXV, no. 4,
1921-1922. Cambridge, 1922).--The conspiracy dilemma:
prosecution of group crime or protection of individual
defendants. (Reprinted from Harvard law review, v. 62,
no. 2, "Notes." Cambridge, 1948).--The logic of
conspiracy. [etc.]
   1. Conspiracy--U. S.--Addresses, essays, lectures.
I. Series.
KF9479.A75L4   345'.73'0231   71-39304
ISBN 0-405-04156-X

CONTENTS

CRIMINAL CONSPIRACY

[Francis B. Sayre]

CRIMINAL CONSPIRACY[1]

IN those fields of industrial controversy where passion runs high and where class conscious groups are arrayed in bitter fight the one against the other, where each side with difficulty is restrained from open war and induced to substitute therefor settlement by judicial action, the law has a very difficult and delicate function to fulfill. Under the terrific thrust and strain of some of the most tremendous social issues of the day, it is of far more than usual importance that the law applicable to labor controversies should express principles of justice evident to and accepted by the great mass of mankind; above all else, such law must be thoroughly predicable. Otherwise class groups will see in legal decisions only the prejudice and bias of the individual judges; and popular respect for the law and its administration by the courts will wane to a possible danger point.

A doctrine so vague in its outlines and uncertain in its fundamental nature as criminal conspiracy lends no strength or glory to the law; it is a veritable quicksand of shifting opinion and ill-considered thought.[2] That this uncertain doctrine should be seized upon, perhaps because of its very vagueness, as one of the principal legal weapons with which lawyers press their attack in labor controversies and in which judges find an easy and frequent support

---

[1] A most admirable book dealing with the subject of Criminal Conspiracy is that of R. S. WRIGHT, THE LAW OF CRIMINAL CONSPIRACIES (London, 1873). This has been much relied on in the preparation of this article.

A scholarly account of the early historical development of Conspiracy has just been published as one of the Cambridge Studies in English Legal History, by P. H. WINFIELD, THE HISTORY OF CONSPIRACY AND ABUSE OF LEGAL PROCEDURE (1921), reviewed in 35 HARV. L. REV. 353.

[2] "The offence of conspiracy," says Mr. Sergeant Talfourd, "is more difficult to be ascertained precisely than any other for which indictment lies; and is, indeed, rather to be considered as governed by positive decisions than by any consistent and intelligible principles of law." Talfourd's edition of DICKINSON'S QUARTER SESSIONS, p. 200 (quoted by Wharton in 3 CRIMINAL LAW, 6 ed., p. 47, note (d). "The law of conspiracy is certainly in a very unsettled state. The decisions have gone on no distinctive principle; nor are they always consistent." C. J. Gibson in Mifflin v. Commonwealth, 5 Watts & S. (Pa.) 461 (1843).

for their decisions is nothing short of a misfortune. It would seem, therefore, of transcendent importance that judges and legal scholars should go to the heart of this matter, and, with eyes resolutely fixed upon justice, should reach some common and definite understanding of the true nature and precise limits of the elusive law of criminal conspiracy.

I

The origin of the crime of conspiracy goes back to the very early pages of the history of our common law. Apparently it grew out of the effort of reformers to correct the abuses of ancient criminal procedure. During the thirteenth century, according to Bracton,[3] there were two modes of commencing prosecution for felonies — the one, by way of private appeal, generally involving trial by battle, and the other by way of public inquest before what later developed into the grand jury. False appeal was in a measure guarded against by the personal liabilities of the appellor; if the appellor were vanquished in the battle by which the truth of the accusation was tried, he was, in the words of Bracton, "committed to gaol, to be punished as a calumniator, but he shall not lose his life nor a limb, although according to the law he is liable to retaliation."[4] Furthermore, the vanquished was liable to a pecuniary penalty. "But upon the duel being finished a penalty of sixty shillings shall be imposed upon the vanquished party as a recreant, and besides he shall lose the law of the land (legem terrae amittet)."[5]

Nevertheless, abuses sprang up; children under twelve, who could not be outlawed and against whom no damages could be recovered, were sometimes incited to bring the appeal. The newer procedure of "indictment upon common report" by a grand jury lent itself to still greater abuse; one could bring to the jury false reports, and thus perhaps accomplish the downfall of his enemy,

---

[3] BRACTON: DE LEGIBUS ET CONSUETUDINIBUS ANGLIAE, f. 143. Compare GLANVILLE: DE LEGIBUS, bk. 14, ch. 1. For the brief survey of the criminal procedure of this period, see 1 STEPHEN, HISTORY OF CRIMINAL LAW, ch. 8; 1 PIKE, HISTORY OF CRIME, ch. 2.

[4] BRACTON, DE LEGIBUS ET CONSUETUDINIBUS ANGLIAE, f. 137.

[5] GLANVILLE, DE LEGIBUS, bk. 2, ch. 3. See also 2 POLLOCK & MAITLAND, HISTORY OF THE ENGLISH LAW, 457, 538.

without incurring the personal risk dependent upon the outcome of the trial by battle. It soon became evident that measures must be taken to correct such practices. For this purpose there was passed in 1285 the statute of 13 Edw. I, c. 12, to the following effect:

"Forasmuch as many, through Malice intending to grieve other, do procure false Appeals to be made of Homicides and other Felonies by Appellors, having nothing wherewith to make Satisfaction to the King for their false Appeal, nor to the Parties appealed for their Damages; it is ordained, That when any, so appealed of Felony surmised upon him, doth acquit himself in the King's Court in Due Manner, either at the Suit of the Appellor, or of our Lord the King, the Justices, before whom such Appeal shall be heard and determined, shall punish the Appellor by one year's Imprisonment; and such Appellors shall nevertheless restore to the Parties appealed their Damages, according to the Discretion of the Justices, having respect to the Imprisonment or Arrestment that the Party appealed hath sustained, by reason of such Appeals, and to the Infamy that they have incurred by the Imprisonment or otherwise: and shall nevertheless make a grievous Fine unto the King. . . ."

Other statutes were passed allowing recovery by writ out of chancery,[6] and by inquest without writ.[7] This series of statutes culminated in the famous Third Ordinance of Conspirators, 33 Edw. I, passed in 1304, which in certain respects summed up the pre-existing law and gave a precise definition of conspiracy:

---

[6] First Ordinance of Conspirators, TOMLIN'S STAT. AT L., 20 EDW. I, p. 399. "Our Lord the King [by] *Gilbert de Roubery*, Clerk of his Council, hath commanded that who ever will complain of Conspirators, Inventors and Maintainers of false quarrels and their Abettors and Supporters and having Part therein, and Brokers of Debates, [that Persons so grieved and complaining shall come to the Chief Justices of our Lord the King, and shall have a Writ of them, under their Seals, to attach such Offenders, to answer to the Parties grieved so complaining before the aforesaid Justices; and such shall be the Writ made for them]. . . . And if any be thereof convicted at the Suit of such Complainants, he shall be imprisoned till he hath made Satisfaction to the Party grieved, and shall also pay a grievous Fine to the King."

[7] Second Ordinance of Conspirators, 28 EDW. I, c. 10 (1300). "In regard to Conspirators, false Informers, and evil Procurers of Dozens, Assises, Inquests and Juries, the King hath ordained Remedy for the Plaintiffs by a Writ out of the Chancery. And notwithstanding, he willeth that his Justices of the one Bench and of the other, and Justices assigned to take Assises, when they come into the Country to do their Office, shall, upon every Plaint made unto them, award Inquests thereupon without Writ, and without Delay, and shall do Right unto the Plaintiffs."

"Conspirators be they that do confeder or bind themselves by Oath, Covenant, or other Alliance, that every of them shall aid and support the Enterprise of each other falsely and maliciously to indite, or cause to be indited [or falsely to acquit people] or falsely to move or maintain Pleas; and also such as cause Children within Age to appeal Men of Felony, whereby they are imprisoned and sore grieved; and such as retain Men with their Liveries or Fees for to maintain their malicious Enterprises; [and to suppress the truth] as well the Takers as the Givers. And Stewards and Bailiffs of great Lords, which, by their Seignory, Office, or Power, undertake to maintain or support [Quarrels, Pleas, or Debates] [for other Matters] than such as touch the Estate of their Lords or themselves.

"[This Ordinance and final Definition of Conspirators was made and finally accorded by the King and his Council in his Parliament the thirty-third Year of his Reign. . . .]"

Finally, the Statute of 4 Edw. III, c. 11 (1330), made conspiracy an offense open to ready prosecution, by providing that the justices of either bench or of assize in sessions "shall enquire, hear, and determine, as well at the King's Suit, as at the Suit of the Party," cases of conspiracy or maintenance "as Justices in Eyre should do if they were in the same county."

Thus, it will be seen that the offense of conspiracy did not originate as a general offense at common law, nor under Norman institutions, but in a series of statutes dating from the time of Edward I, enacted to remedy a specific abuse. The statutes themselves make clear how narrow and restricted was the early offense of conspiracy. The offense admitted of no broad common-law generalizations; it was limited to offenses against the administration of justice, and was strictly confined to the precise and definite language of the statutes. Combinations only to procure false indictments or to bring false appeals or to maintain vexatious suits could constitute conspiracies.[8]

---

[8] "The earliest meaning of conspiracy was thus a combination to carry on legal proceedings in a vexatious or improper way, and the writ of conspiracy, and the power given by the *Articuli super Chartas* to proceed without such a writ, were the forerunners of our modern actions for malicious prosecution. Originally, therefore, conspiracy was rather a particular kind of civil injury than a substantive crime, but like many other civil injuries it was also punishable on indictment, at the suit of the king, and upon a conviction the offender was liable to an extremely severe punishment which was called 'the villain judgment.'" 2 STEPHEN, HIST. OF THE CRIM. LAW, 228.

We have the record of a case decided in 1351 [9] wherein the court was called upon to decide whether the offense of conspiracy could be so broadened as to include combinations to commit acts of a generally illegal and oppressive nature. Upon a presentment of conspiracy in the Eyre of Derby grounded upon allegations that the defendants had imprisoned and generally oppressed the people, a judgment had been rendered against the defendants; and one of the defendants then sought to reverse the judgment of the lower court. Justice Shardelowe, pressed to brand the defendant's conduct as a conspiracy, stoutly refused; and, in spite of the arguments of counsel, reversed the former decision, partly because no specific year or day or place had been named in the presentment, and partly "because the principal matter of the conspiracy alleged is not conspiracy, but rather damage and oppression of the people." Although between the reigns of Edward III and Elizabeth a number of statutes were passed to suppress combinations for various specific purposes, such as treasonable designs, breaches of the peace, raising prices, and the like, yet prior to the seventeenth century there seems to have been no mention of any combination or confederacy having been held criminal under the common law except the crime of conspiracy as defined by the Ordinance of 1305.[10]

According to the older notions, the crime of conspiracy for procuring false indictments was not complete until the person falsely accused had been actually indicted and acquitted.[11] Nothing short of an acquittal following an indictment would do.[12] This seems to

---

[9] Anon., Year Book, 24 Edw. III, f. 75, pl. 99.

[10] It is to be noted, however, that by the early part of the sixteenth century the courts had developed a common-law "Action upon the Case for a Conspiracy" for damages for cases of procuring false indictments where the facts would not strictly support a case under the Conspiracy Writs, as for example, where a single person had procured a false indictment. See Fitzherbert, Natura Brevium, 114 D. See also the case of Marsh v. Vauhan, Cro. Eliz. 701. In that case two had been indicted for conspiracy, and one was found guilty and the other not. The court thereupon quashed the indictment; and the opinion of the whole court was "that a writ of conspiracy lies not, nor is maintainable upon this verdict. But an action upon the case, in nature of a conspiracy, might have been brought in this case."

[11] Where the conspiracy was for maintenance, however, it had been held as early as 1354 that the defendants might be held to answer for the conspiracy each to maintain the other though no suit had actually been commenced. See Anon., 27 Ass., f. 138 b, pl. 44.

[12] "A Writ of Conspiracy lieth where two, three or more persons of malice and covin do conspire and devise to indict any person falsely, and afterwards he who is so

have remained the well-settled law for some three centuries; it was not until the close of the sixteenth century that the courts began to relax the strictness with which they had always limited the crime of conspiracy. During the reign of James I, Chief Justice Popham recalled a case, decided in 1574, wherein the justices had suggested that a common-law indictment for conspiracy might be allowed against false accusers even though no indictment upon the false charge had been found by the grand jury.[13] Such a doctrine was authoritatively established by the Court of Star Chamber in the famous *Poulterers' Case*,[14] decided in 1611. Thus was taken the first step in the long process by which the early rigidly defined crime of conspiracy was, through judicial, analogical extension, gradually expanded into the vague and uncertain doctrine which we know to-day.

In the *Poulterers' Case*, the defendant poulterers had confederated to bring against one, Stone, a false accusation of robbery; but Stone was so manifestly innocent of the crime charged that the grand jury refused to indict him. As a defense to the action for damages subsequently brought by Stone against his false accusers, it was argued that since he had never been indicted or acquitted, no recovery could be had; "because no writ of conspiracy for the party grieved, or indictment or other suit for the King lies, but where the party grieved is indicted, and *legitimo modo acquietatus*, as the books are F. N. B. 114b; 6 E. 3, 41a; 24 E. 3, 34b; 43 E. 3. Conspiracy 11; 27 Ass., p. 59; 19 H. 6, 28; 21 H. 6, 26; 9 E. 4, 12, &c." But the Court of Star Chamber squarely decided to the contrary, citing certain early notes, and definitely held that, as in conspiracies for maintenance, the confederating together constituted the gist of the offense rather than the false indictment and subsequent acquittal. From the doctrine announced by this

---

indicted is acquitted; now he shall have this Writ of Conspiracy against them who so indicted him." FITZHERBERT, NATURA BREVIUM, 114 D. Coke defines conspiracy as "a consultation and agreement between two or more to appeale or indict an innocent falsely and maliciously of felony, whom accordingly they cause to be indicted and appealed; and afterward the party is lawfully acquitted by the verdict of twelve men." (3 INST. 142–143.) So, Hudson, in his treatise on the Star Chamber (2 COLL. JURID. 104, 105) says in regard to conspiracy: "But when the party is indicted, and not *legitimo modo acquietatus*, then can no conspiracy lie, as it was adjudged in *Daniel Wright's* case." See also Sherington *v.* Ward, Cro. Eliz. 724.

[13] Sydenham *v.* Keilaway, Cro. Jac. 7.

[14] 9 Coke 55 b.

decision, it was an easy step to the very general doctrine that since the gist of the crime is the conspiracy, no other overt act is necessary; [15] and this came to be the well-acknowledged law of criminal conspiracy.[16] In the ancient phraseology, it was not necessary to show that anything had been "put in ure"; [17] the mere conspiracy alone was held to constitute the gist of the offense and to be therefore indictable. There seems to be no doubt but that the courts in adopting this doctrine followed a sound instinct; and the principle, thus early decided, has come to be a universal and well-settled doctrine of the modern law of conspiracy. There is nothing in the doctrine out of accord with the well-recognized principle of criminal law that without some overt act no one can be convicted of a common-law crime, no matter how black his intent may have been. For the conspiring together itself constitutes an overt act which may well furnish the basis of criminal liability. Once given some overt act, the criminal law does not necessarily require the fulfillment of the defendant's designs or the completion of his intended actions before liability attaches. The entire law of attempts bears witness to the contrary.

Some writers, indeed, have viewed the law of criminal conspiracy as an outgrowth of the larger law of criminal attempts.[18] That the two have many features in common and are based very largely on the same general underlying principles, cannot be gainsaid. Nevertheless, the two are not to-day the same; every criminal conspiracy is not an attempt. One may become guilty of conspiracy long before his act has come so dangerously near to completion as to make him criminally liable for the attempted crime.

---

[15] The growth of this doctrine may be traced in the following cases: Rex v. Kimberty, 1 Lev. 62 (1663); Rex v. Armstrong, 1 Ventr. 304 (1678); Rex v. Best, 2 Ld. Raym. 1167, 6 Mod. 185 (1705); Rex v. Kinnersley & Moore, 1 Stra. 193 (1719).

[16] See, for example, 1 HAWKINS, PLEAS OF THE CROWN, c. 72, § 2. As Hawkins points out, a distinction was drawn between a formal action based upon the writ of conspiracy and "an action on the case in the nature of such writ."

[17] Anon., 27 Ass., f. 138 b, pl. 44 (1354).

[18] See, for example, WRIGHT, LAW OF CONSPIRACY, 36, 62. Stephen also comments on the analogy between the law of conspiracy and that of attempts. 2 STEPHEN, HISTORY OF THE CRIMINAL LAW, 227. Bishop goes so far as to say: "The act of conspiring, and the specific intent to accomplish what constitutes a substantive crime, are in combination a criminal attempt, and it is the professional usage to term it conspiracy. It follows the same rules, and is subject to the same limitations, as other attempts." 2 BISHOP, NEW CRIM. LAW, 8 ed., § 191(2), p. 107. "It is not called in the books 'attempt,' but it is such in nature and effect." (1 Ibid., § 592.)

For instance, as Justice Holmes has pointed out, the mere agreement to murder a man fifty miles away could not possibly constitute an attempt, but might easily be indictable as a conspiracy.[19]

During the seventeenth century the courts took a second step in extending and broadening the limits of the crime of conspiracy of even greater importance than the one just described. Prior to this century, the crime had been confined very strictly to combinations to defeat the just administration of the law, such as the procuring of false indictments, embracery, and maintenance. During the seventeenth century the courts began to extend the offense so as to cover combinations to commit all crimes of whatsoever nature, misdemeanors as well as felonies.[20] This was a bold extension indeed. It was due in part to the abolition of the Court of Star Chamber, which cast upon the Court of King's Bench the duty, hitherto assumed by the Star Chamber, of dealing with misdemeanors; and the judges of King's Bench, groping their way through unfamiliar paths, tried new legal adventures. Perhaps it was due even more largely to the character of the period or stage through which the law was passing. People had felt the injustice of the hard, narrow formalism, the rigidity and unjust technicalities of the "Strict Law" period of the fourteenth, fifteenth, and sixteenth centuries. During the seventeenth and eighteenth centuries a reaction set in, in favor of a broader, more moral law. Finespun intricacies of pleading and the technicalities of formal writs began to give way before questions of right and wrong. It was a period when the courts were busy infusing morals into the law; and inevitably, as part of this process of infusion, there came to be a blurring of the line of distinction between law and morals, and a consequent confusion of the two. In 1616, in *Bagg's Case*,[21] the Court of King's Bench formally "resolved, that to this Court of King's Bench belongs authority, not only to correct errors in judicial proceedings, but other errors and misdemeanors extrajudicial, tending to the breach of peace, or oppression of the subjects, or to the raising of faction, controversy, debate, or to any

---

[19] Hyde *v.* United States, 225 U. S. 347, 388 (1912).

[20] The courts of this period even went so far as to hold criminal a combination to accuse one of an offense cognizable only in the spiritual courts. See Rex *v.* Timberley & Childe, 1 Sid. 68, 1 Keb. 203, 254 (1663).

[21] 11 Co. Rep. 93 b, 98 a (1616).

manner of misgovernment; so that no wrong or injury, either public or private, can be done, but that it shall be (here) reformed or punished by due course of law." So in *Rex* v. *Sidney*,[22] decided in 1664, twenty-four years after the abolition of the Court of Star Chamber, the Court of King's Bench, addressing the defendant indicted for several misdemeanors, "which were a great scandal of Christianity," reiterated much the same doctrine, declaring that "although there was not now a Star Chamber, still they would have him know that this court is *custos morum* of all the subjects of the King." Even as late as Lord Mansfield's time, such pretensions had not been entirely abandoned. In the case of *Jones* v. *Randall*,[23] Lord Mansfield re-echoed good seventeenth-century doctrine when he said: "Whatever is *contra bonos mores et decorum*, the principles of our law prohibit, and the King's Court, as the general censor and guardian of the public manners, is bound to restrain and punish."

Hence, during the latter part of the seventeenth century, when the tendency of the courts was in the direction of undertaking to punish acts immoral as well as those violative of express law, it was not strange that the idea should gain currency on many sides that courts should similarly undertake to punish conspiracies to commit immoral as well as those to commit illegal acts. The idea that a combination may be criminal, although its object would not be strictly criminal apart from the combination, first began to take articulate form towards the close of the seventeenth century in the arguments of counsel. Nevertheless, the judges stoutly refused to follow such suggestions. The doctrine seems to have been squarely repudiated by Lord Holt in 1704;[24] in fact, during the whole of the seventeenth century, when the courts were stretching and liberalizing legal principles and doctrines to extremely wide limits, there seems to be no evidence of a single case (apart from the doubtful exception of *Starling's Case*[25]) where the courts

---

[22] 1 Sid. 168 (1664).   [23] Lofft, 383 (1774).

[24] Daniell's Case, 6 Mod. 99, 1 Salk. 380 (1704).

[25] Rex *v.* Starling, 1 Sid. 174 (1665). But apparently even in this case the defendants were convicted because of the criminal nature of what they were conspiring to do, *i. e.*, to interfere with the farming of the public revenues. As Lord Holt said in Reg. *v.* Daniell, 6 Mod. 99, 100, "the case of Starling was directly of a publick nature, and levelled at the government; and the gist of the offense was its influence on the publick. . . ."

allowed a conspiracy conviction for a combination to commit an act not itself criminal.[26]

After the seventeenth century, when the courts receded from their extreme seventeenth-century pretensions, the indefensible doctrine suggested by arguing counsel might well have been forgotten had it not been for an unfortunately ambiguous statement made by Hawkins in his *Pleas of the Crown*, published in 1716. Concerning the crime of conspiracy, Hawkins said: "There can be no doubt, but that all confederacies whatsoever, wrongfully to prejudice a third person, are highly criminal at common law." [27]

What did Hawkins mean by "wrongfully"? If he meant by criminal means it was exceedingly unfortunate that he did not choose terms confined to such a meaning; if he meant by tortious or merely immoral means, the authorities which he cites in support of his statement by no means sustain him,[28] and almost his only support is to be found in the loose *dicta* of seventeenth-century courts and in the arguments of counsel. Nevertheless, Hawkins' erroneous statement lived on, partly because of the acknowledged authority of the writer, partly because of the seventeenth and eighteenth century confusion of law and morals, partly because of the very ambiguity of the statement which rendered it the less liable to be challenged and the more difficult to disprove. In the

---

[26] WRIGHT, LAW OF CONSPIRACY, 67.

[27] HAWKINS, PLEAS OF THE CROWN, 6 ed., bk. 1, c. 72, § 2, p. 348.

[28] Hawkins cites in support of his statement only four cases and two notes. These are Rex *v.* Timberley, 1 Sid. 68, 1 Keb. 254, 1 Lev. 62; The Poulterers' Case, 9 Coke 55 b; Reg. *v.* Best, 6 Mod. 185; and Starling's Case, 1 Lev. 125, 126, 1 Sid. 174; 1 Keb. 650; and the two brief notes in 27 Ass. 44 (6) and 2 Rol. Ab. 77 pl. 2, 3. (Two of Hawkins' citations are erroneous. For 1 Keble 350, he evidently means 1 Keble 650, and for 1 Mod. 185, he evidently means 6 Mod. 185). With the possible exception of Starling's Case, not one of these cases or notes supports Hawkins' statement. All except Starling's Case fall within the terms of the Ordinances of Conspirators or are conspiracies to achieve some criminal object, and therefore prove nothing as to the criminality at common law of a "confederacy wrongfully to prejudice a third person." Rex *v.* Timberley and The Poulterers' Case concern conspiracies to procure false indictments; Reg *v.* Best concerns a conspiracy falsely to charge another with being the father of a bastard in order to extort money. Even the two notes do not support Hawkins' statement. Hawkins' only possible support is Starling's Case; and a careful reading of that case would seem to prove exactly the opposite of Hawkins' statement. As Wright states (LAW OF CRIMINAL CONSPIRACY, p. 38): "[Starling's Case] appears to amount to a decision that a combination to impoverish a man (other than the king) by means not criminal in themselves, is not criminal."

course of time, the statement came to be regarded as authoritative and thus furnished the foundation of later *dicta* and judicial opinion.

From this time on, the well-acknowledged formula that the conspiracy constitutes the gist of the offense came to be infused with quite a new meaning in order to support the statement of Hawkins interpreted in its erroneous sense. In the case of *Rex v. Edwards*, [29] decided in 1724, eight years after the publication of Hawkins' book, certain defendants were indicted for having entered into a conspiracy to marry off a pauper woman to the inhabitant of another parish so that their own parish might escape further liability for her support. The counsel indulged in the usual arguments, the defense insisting that no one could be convicted for conspiring to achieve something not a crime, and the prosecution, quite regardless of any distinction between law and morals, arguing that "a conspiracy to do a lawful act, if it be for a bad end, is a good foundation for an indictment." The decision, it is true, was correctly rendered for the defendant; but the court by way of *dictum* echoed the loose ideas of Hawkins, stating that a "bare conspiracy to do a lawful act to an unlawful end is a crime, though no act be done in consequence thereof," citing as its only authority *Reg. v. Best*, [30] which in reality lends no support to the doctrine that one can be convicted for conspiring to commit some illegal but non-criminal act.

Another case often quoted in support of the Hawkins doctrine is *Rex v. Journeymen Tailors*,[31] decided in 1721, where certain journeymen tailors were indicted and found guilty of a conspiracy to raise their wages. In the course of the opinion the court is reported as saying that "a conspiracy of any kind is illegal, although the matter about which they conspired might have been lawful for them, or any of them, to do, if they had not conspired to do it, as appears in the case of *The Tubwomen v. The Brewers of London*." A careful search of the authorities has failed to reveal the existence of any such case as the one cited. Those who rely upon *Rex v. Journeymen Tailors* as a support for the Hawkins doctrine forget that at the time of the decision there was in force in England a

[29] 8 Mod. 320 (1724).
[30] 6 Mod. 185; 2 Ld. Ray. 1167 (1705).
[31] 8 Mod. 10 (1721).

statute,[32] passed the preceding year, which expressly made it criminal for journeymen tailors to enter into any agreement "for advancing their Wages or for lessening their usual Hours of Work"; under this statute and under 2 & 3 Edw. 6, c. 15, the defendants' conduct would have been criminal quite apart from any conspiracy doctrine.

Apart from the fraud cases, where the Hawkins doctrine crept into the decisions during the latter part of the seventeenth and the early eighteenth centuries, and from which it has never been eliminated, the vast majority of actual decisions still continued to adhere to the long-established law that there could be no conspiracy conviction unless the object conspired for or the means used was criminal. For instance, in the much-quoted case of *Rex* v. *Turner*,[33] decided by the King's Bench in 1811, an indictment was brought for conspiracy for "unlawfully and wickedly devising and intending to injure, oppress and aggrieve" a certain property-owner by "unlawfully and wickedly" conspiring to poach upon his preserve for hares with "divers bludgeons and other offensive weapons," and for breaking into the said preserve and "carrying into execution their unlawful and wicked purposes." The prosecution relied on the now familiar arguments, quoting in support of their position both Hawkins and *Rex* v. *Edwards*. But Lord Ellenborough would have none of such arguments, and made absolute a rule to arrest the judgment upon a verdict of guilty, saying: "I should be sorry to have it doubted whether persons agreeing to go and sport upon another's ground, in other words, to commit a civil trespass, should be thereby in peril of an indictment for an offence which would subject them to infamous punishment."

Nevertheless, in spite of square decisions, such as *Rex* v. *Turner*, holding that combinations to commit non-criminal acts cannot apart from statute themselves be criminal, the seventeenth-century ideas persisted. Now and again in arguments of counsel, in *dicta*, in epigrammatic statements, in occasional actual decisions,

---

[32] 7 GEO. I, c. 13, p. 403 (1720). This statute fixed the daily hours of work for journeymen tailors as running from six o'clock in the morning to eight o'clock at night; the wages were fixed from March 25 to June 24 at "any sum not exceeding Two Shillings per Diem, and for the Rest of the Year One Shilling and Eight Pence per Diem."

[33] 13 East, 228 (1811).

the ghost of Hawkins still walked. Hawkins' language was literally adopted and transcribed into Burn's *Justice*,[34] which was first published in 1755 and which, in succeeding editions, was so widely read during the eighteenth and nineteenth centuries. It was also copied into Wilson's *Works*.[35] Chitty, in his *Criminal Law*,[36] again repeats the Hawkins formula, saying: "In a word, all confederacies wrongfully to prejudice another are misdemeanors at common law, whether the intention is to injure his property, his person, or his character." And in Christian's edition of Blackstone's *Commentaries*,[37] it is said: "Every confederacy to injure individuals, or to do acts which are unlawful, or prejudicial to the community, is a conspiracy." A reincarnation of the doctrine took form in Lord Denman's famous epigram that a conspiracy indictment must "charge a conspiracy either to do an unlawful act or a lawful act by unlawful means." [38]

Like the magic jingle in some fairy tale, through whose potency the bewitched adventurer is delivered from all his troubles, this famous formula was seized upon by judges laboring bewildered through the mazes of the conspiracy cases as a ready solution for all their difficulties. It would fit any conspiracy case whatever; it was, so to speak, ready to wear, and obviated the necessity of carefully thinking through or correctly analyzing the doctrine of conspiracy. As a consequence, judges gave to it the widest use. In spite of the fact that Lord Denman himself later apparently repudiated it,[39] it came to be considered as a sacred and final dispensation of the law. The real difficulty was that it contained the same kind of ambiguity as did Hawkins' statement in the preceding century; "unlawful" might be interpreted so as to mean "criminal," in which case it correctly stated the law according to the great majority of decisions; or it might

---

[34] 1 RICHARD BURN, THE JUSTICE OF THE PEACE, 4 ed., p. 276.

[35] 3 JAMES WILSON, WORKS, 118.   [36] Vol. 3, 1 ed., p. 1139.

[37] Vol. 4, p. 136 (Christian's note 4).

[38] See Jones' Case, 4 B. & Ad. 345, 349 (1832). Wright, in speaking of this famous statement says (LAW OF CRIM. CONSPIRACY, p. 63): "That antithesis was invented by Lord Denman . . . to express the very opposite of that for which it is sometimes cited." Compare Rex v. Seward, 1 A. & E. 706, 711, 713 (1834).

[39] In the subsequent case of Reg. v. Peck, 9 A. & E. 686, 690 (1839) Lord Denman said in reply to counsel quoting his own words to him: "I do not think the antithesis very correct."

without doing the least violence to the language, be interpreted to include "tortious" as well as "criminal," in which case eighteenth-century misconceptions would be still further perpetuated. Unfortunately, it was in the latter sense that it was too often interpreted, particularly in the loose *dicta* of the conspiracy cases.

The truth of the matter is that judges found the Hawkins conception of criminal conspiracy entirely too convenient an instrument for enforcing their own individual notions of justice to be lightly discarded. It enabled judges to punish by criminal process such concerted conduct as seemed to them socially oppressive or undesirable, even though the actual deeds committed constituted of themselves no crime, either by statute or by common law. And in cases where the actual deeds were of doubtful criminality, it saved the judges from the often embarrassing necessity of having to spell out the crime.

Illustrations of this among the nineteenth-century cases are not difficult to find. Thus, in *Rex* v. *Bykerdike*,[40] decided in 1832, the defendants were indicted for conspiracy for threatening a strike among the employees in a certain colliery unless certain other employees should be discharged. The action was brought after the Combinations Act of 1800 [41] had been repealed; and it was popularly supposed that the effect of the Acts of 1824 [42] and 1825 [43] had been to free labor unions from the charge of criminality which had attached to them under the former Combinations Act. Quite possibly in *Rex* v. *Bykerdyke*, the separate acts of the defendants, apart from conspiracy, might have been held to be criminal under the very ambiguous words of the Act of 1825, which prohibited in trade disputes a "molesting or in any way obstructing another." But the point is that the judge apparently never took the trouble to define, nor so far as appears from the report, to inquire into the precise meaning of these ambiguous words; instead he held the defendants as criminals under a vague conspiracy doctrine without any discussion or indication as to whether under the Act of 1825 criminality attached to the means they used or the object they sought, or both, or neither. The jury were informed simply that "a conspiracy to procure the discharge of any of the work-

---

[40] 1 Mood. & Rob. 179 (1832).

[41] 40 GEO. III, c. 106.

[42] 5 GEO. IV, c. 95.

[43] 6 GEO. IV, c. 129.

men would support the indictment. . . ." [44] The case illustrates, not necessarily a faulty decision, but the obvious convenience and consequent danger of a doctrine which will allow a judge to enforce by criminal punishment his individual ideas of what makes for or against the social welfare.

Similar illustrations are to be found among the American cases. In *State* v. *Donaldson*,[45] several employees had been indicted upon a conspiracy charge for notifying their employer that unless he discharged certain other employees, they would quit his employment. After a careful examination of the case, the court could find nothing criminal in the separate acts committed by the defendants. Nevertheless, relying partly upon *Rex* v. *Bykerdyke*,[46] and one other English case,[47] it refused to quash the indictment; and it proceeded to brand the defendants as criminals because of their participation in a combination which it regarded as illegal and criminal by reason of its generally oppressive nature. The court said:[48] "It may safely be said, nevertheless, that a combination will be an indictable conspiracy . . . where the confederacy, having no lawful aim, tends simply to the oppression of individuals." When and under what principles action which otherwise constitutes no violation of the criminal law may be said to be criminal because it "tends to the oppression of individuals" is a question upon which the court remained discreetly silent. The conduct of those who go on strike to compel their employer to discharge other non-union employees is clearly not criminal apart from any conspiracy doctrine. Indeed, in the majority of states it is held not even tortious.[49] Acts "tending to the oppression of

---

[44] The Judge's only reference to the Act of 1825 was the last sentence of the opinion in which he said that, "the statute never meant to empower workmen to meet and combine for the purpose of dictating to the master whom he should employ, and that this compulsion was clearly illegal." But this summary reference leaves entirely undecided whether the criminality lay in the combination, or in some "molesting" of employees, or in some "obstructing" of the employer.

[45] 32 N. J. L. 151 (1867).

[46] The court quite disregarded or overlooked the fact that Rex *v.* Bykerdyke was decided under the English Act of 1825 which made criminal the "molesting or in any way obstructing another" in a trade dispute, — a statute which of course was not in force in New Jersey.

[47] See *Ibid.*, 156, 157.   [48] *Ibid.*, p. 154.

[49] See, for instance, Cohn & Roth Electric Co. *v.* Bricklayers' Union, 92 Conn. 161, 101 Atl. 659 (1917); Jetton-Dekle Lumber Co. *v.* Mather, 53 Fla. 969, 43 So. 590 (1907);

individuals" committed in other fields of trade competition have often been held entirely justifiable.[50] Yet in *State* v. *Donaldson*, Chief Justice Beasley held that defendants joining in such a strike were actual criminals.[51] Perhaps no case could better illustrate the vague menace of a criminal-law doctrine by means of which conduct usually regarded as perfectly lawful, and nowhere, apart from the conspiracy doctrine, regarded as criminal, can be turned by a judge who happens to be out of sympathy with the defendants' efforts into a criminal offense.

In *State* v. *Burnham*,[52] decided in 1844, a New Hampshire Court went so far as to declare that a combination to commit a merely immoral act might constitute a criminal conspiracy. Justice Gilchrist said:

"An act may be immoral without being indictable, where the isolated acts of an individual are not so injurious to society as to require the intervention of the law. But when immoral acts are committed by numbers, in furtherance of a common object, and with the advantages and strength which determination and union impart to them, they assume the grave importance of a conspiracy, and the peace and order of society require their repression. . . . When it is said in the books that the means must be unlawful, it is not to be understood that those means must amount to indictable offences, in order to make the offence of conspiracy

---

Kemp v. Division, No. 241, 255 Ill. 213, 99 N. E. 389 (1912); Clemmitt v. Watson, 14 Ind. App. 38, 42 N. E. 367 (1895); Gray v. Bldg. Trades Council, 91 Minn. 171, 185, 97 N. W. 663 (1903); State v. Employers of Labor, 102 Neb. 768, 774, 169 N. W. 768 (1918); National Protective Ass'n v. Cumming, 170 N. Y. 315, 63 N. E. 369 (1902); Kissam v. United States Printing Co. 199 N. Y. 76, 92 N. E. 214 (1910); Bossert v. Dhuy, 221 N. Y. 342, 117 N. E. 582 (1917); State v. Van Pelt, 136 N. C. 633, 49 S. E. 177 (1904); Roddy v. United Mine Workers, 41 Okla. 621, 139 Pac. 126 (1914); Sheehan v. Levy, 215 S. W. 229 (Tex. Civ. App., 1919). *Contra*: Plant v. Woods, 176 Mass. 492, 57 N. E. 1011 (1899), and numerous other Massachusetts cases; Ruddy v. Plumbers, 79 N. J. L. 467, 75 Atl. 742 (1910); Bausbach v. Reiff, 244 Pa. 559, 91 Atl. 224 (1914); State v. Dyer, 67 Vt. 690, 32 Atl. 814 (1894).

[50] Mogul Steamship Co. v. McGregor, [1892] A. C. 25; Macauley Bros. v. Tierney, 19 R. I. 255, 33 Atl. 1 (1895); Bohn Mfg. Co. v. Hollis, 54 Minn. 223, 55 N. W. 1119 (1893).

[51] In the later New Jersey case of Jersey City Printing Co. v. Cassidy, 63 N. J. Eq. 759, 762, 53 Atl. 230 (1902), the Court said: "The doctrine of the old cases, of which we have in New Jersey an interesting example in *State* v. *Donaldson* . . . which placed the employee, when acting in combination with his fellow-workmen, at a tremendous disadvantage as compared with his employer, I think may be regarded as entirely exploded."

[52] 15 N. H. 396, 402, 403 (1844).

complete. It will be enough if they are corrupt, dishonest, fraudulent, immoral, and in that sense illegal, and it is in the combination to make use of such practices that the dangers of this offence consist."

Such language sounds more as though it had been written by the Court of Star Chamber in the seventeenth century than by a judge in liberty-loving America more than half a century after the American Revolution. Yet in spite of the fact that the doctrine of *State* v. *Burnham* was apparently directly overruled in the later New Hampshire case of *State* v. *Straw*,[53] *State* v. *Burnham* is still quoted to-day in support of the Hawkins doctrine.[54] Thus, like an underground stream that ever keeps coming to the surface, the doctrine, constantly reiterated in the loose *dicta* of courts and the statements of text-writers, has kept appearing and reappearing ever since Hawkins' time, in spite of the fact that, apart from fraud cases, so far as actual decisions are concerned the doctrine finds almost no support.[55]

II

Thus far the doctrine that a combination to commit a non-criminal act may constitute a criminal conspiracy has been examined solely from the historical viewpoint; and in the light of history the doctrine seems so manifestly founded upon misconceptions and erroneous applications of ambiguous statements that it is difficult to support. But many wholesome and salutary doctrines of the law have sprung up through misunderstandings of past decisions or without any historical basis whatsoever. To show the historical illegitimacy of a legal doctrine does not disprove its present right of existence or its usefulness. Quite apart from historical considerations, is the doctrine logically sound? Will it bear the test of careful analytical scrutiny?

An analytical examination of the doctrine raises new difficulties. If the object sought by a combination is in no way criminal, and if the means utilized are in no way criminal, just wherein lies

---

[53] 42 N. H. 393, 396 (5) (1861). The court in this case squarely held that a combination to commit a civil trespass did not constitute a criminal conspiracy.

[54] See, for example, 8 Cyc. 624, note 19; 12 C. J. 548, note 48; 2 Bishop, New Crim. Law, 8 ed., § 181, note 2 (p. 103); 3 Wharton, Crim. Law, 6 ed., 81, note (l), § 2326.

[55] See *infra*, p. 422 *et seq.*

any criminality? The mere act of combining can surely not be criminal, where no criminal end is sought nor criminal means used. It is no crime to combine to form a social club, a church, a political association. As was said by Serjeant Talfourd, in discussing the crime of conspiracy: [56]

"It is not easy to understand on what principle conspiracies have been holden indictable where neither the end nor the means are, in themselves, regarded by the law as criminal, however reprehensible in point of morals. Mere concert is not in itself a crime; for associations to prosecute felons, and even to put laws in force against political offenders, have been holden legal.[57] If, then, there be no indictable offence in the object; no indictable offence in the means; and no indictable offence in the concert, in what part of the conduct of the conspirators is the offence to be found? Can several circumstances, each perfectly lawful, make up an unlawful act? And yet such is the general language held on this subject, that at one time the immorality of the object is relied on; at another, the evidence of the means; while, at all times, the concert is stated to be the essence of the charge; and yet that concert, independent of an illegal object or illegal means, is admitted to be blameless."

The answer which naturally suggests itself to such arguments is that just as in chemistry the combination of A, B, and C, all non-poisonous substances, may form a new compound, D, poisonous and quite different from the elements of which it is composed, so in criminal law separate acts, each alone perfectly lawful, may, when combined together, constitute such an anti-social effect that the actors' conduct as a whole becomes criminal. The mere act of crooking a finger on the trigger of a gun is not of itself necessarily unlawful; neither is there necessarily any criminality in the mere act of pointing a gun, nor in the act of loading one. Yet when all these acts are combined, in certain circumstances the resultant effect may constitute a crime. So, a single man blowing a whistle on the streets at night might constitute no nuisance; but if a hundred men did identically the same thing in combination, they might easily be indictable for creating a public nuisance.

But such an answer does not explain away all of the difficulty.

---

[56] Wm. Dickinson, A Practical Guide to the Quarter Sessions, 3 ed. by T. N. Talfourd (1829), p. 201.

[57] R. *v.* Murray, tried before Abbot, C. J., at Guildhall, 1823; cited in 1 Burn, Justice of the Peace, 30 ed., p. 976.

It leaves unexplained how it is that precisely the same effect which is perfectly lawful when procured by one becomes criminal when procured by two. When closely analyzed, criminality consists, not in detached separate acts, but in the anti-social *effect* of acts.[58] For instance, in the gun case above suggested, murder is committed, not where the finger is crooked upon the trigger, but where the anti-social *effect* of the act takes place, *i. e.*, where the bullet hits the victim's body;[59] and it is this particular anti-social *effect* which is labeled as the crime of murder. To convict a criminal defendant it is not necessary to prove that he was ever physically present or that he acted within the state; it is sufficient to show that the anti-social *effect* of his acts, committed elsewhere with *mens rea*, operated within the state.[60] If criminality then consists, not in mere acts, but in the anti-social effect of acts, must not criminality be measured by the nature of the effect,[61] and not by the character or number of those whose acts produce that effect? For instance, in the nuisance case suggested above, if a single man arranged by steam to blow the same hundred whistles on the street at night, no one would suppose that he would not be indictable for the nuisance. If criminality is to be measured by the character of the *effect* of the defendant's acts, how can it make any possible difference as to criminality whether the identical effect is procured by one or two or a hundred? How then can it be said that if a single individual procures a certain effect by certain means he is not a criminal, but if a combination of individuals procure the self-same effect by the self-same means, they are all criminals? Is such a doctrine logically defensible? [62]

---

[58] Acts being defined, in the words of Mr. Holmes, as voluntary "muscular contractions." — HOLMES, THE COMMON LAW, p. 54.

[59] See, for example, United States *v.* Davis, 2 Sumn. (U. S.) 482 (1837); State *v.* Hall, 114 N. C. 909, 19 S. E. 602 (1894).

[60] Of course it is necessary also to show that the anti-social effect is such as constitutes, under the law of the prosecuting state, a criminal offense.

[61] If, for example, after the defendant had fired at his victim with full intent to kill him, the bullet had been deflected perhaps by another bullet, and the victim not hit, there would have been no crime of murder, although every single act and motive of the defendant would have been precisely the same.

[62] Adherents of the Hawkins doctrine sometimes seek to defend the logic of the doctrine by its analogy to the offenses of routs and riots. Routs and riots are crimes which by common law require the concurrence of three or more persons. No matter how great a tumult a single person may make, he cannot be indicted for a rout or a

III

But the law, which after all exists primarily to achieve justice and thus to promote social peace and equilibrium, must not be bound down too arbitrarily by logical or purely analytical considerations any more than by the iron grip of historical precedents and correctly traced legal genealogies. If the purpose of legal doctrines is to promote the social security and well-being, they must be examined functionally and tested by the degree of protection which they afford to social and to individual interests or rights.

A law which protects must be a predicable law; indeed one of the most essential attributes of all law is predicability. It is perhaps this more than any other factor which makes justice according to law preferable to justice without law, as found for example in legislative or executive justice.[63] The excellence of justice according to law, or judicial justice, rests upon the fact that judges are not free to render decisions based purely upon their personal predilections and peculiar dispositions, no matter how good or how wise they may be; they are bound by principles embodying the accumulated wisdom and experience of past ages, and those principles furnish a fixed standard by which citizens of the state may measure or shape their conduct and by which the course of justice can be reasonably foreseen and predicted. Once rob the law of this predicability, and the state reverts to a government by men rather than by law. No one will be secure in his or her interests

---

riot. But the analogy after all is rather superficial. Criminality, here as elsewhere, is measured by the anti-social effects of the defendants' acts; and in the inherent nature of things it is impossible for a single individual to produce the effect of a riot. In other words, a single person is not indictable for a riot, because it is inherently impossible for him to produce the anti-social effect or criminal consequence known as a riot; but as to cases of conspiracy it is in fact very frequently possible for a single individual to procure or cause identically the same criminal consequence as a combination may procure.

[63] Interesting examples of legislative justice will be found in the judicial powers exercised by American colonial legislatures and state legislatures immediately after the Revolution, such as the issue of bills of attainder, bills of pains and penalties, legislative granting of new trials, legislative divorce proceedings, insolvency proceedings, etc. See POUND, OUTLINES OF LECTURES ON JURISPRUDENCE, 3 ed., p. 75. Legislative justice has generally been recognized as capricious, uncertain, and therefore often unjust and tyrannical, and highly susceptible to prejudice and extra-legal considerations.

or rights, for no one can foretell what interests individual judges may see fit to protect or to disregard. If the criminal law permits judges to determine criminality by their own individual standards and prejudices, we must face again the anxious fears and troubled insecurity of the old Star Chamber days; decisions will lose their predicability, and the law will obviously cease to protect.

If a legal doctrine is to be tested functionally according to the degree of security which it affords to the individual and social interests which the law was created to protect, any doctrine which tends to rob the law of its predicability, therefore, must be accounted pernicious. It is hard to imagine a doctrine which would more effectively rob the law of predicability so far as it is applicable than the one that a criminal conspiracy includes combinations to do anything against the general moral sense of the community. Under such a principle every one who acts in co-operation with another may some day find his liberty dependent upon the innate prejudices or social bias of an unknown judge. It is the very antithesis of justice according to law. There will be a very real danger of courts being invoked, especially during periods of reaction, to punish, as criminal, associations which for the time being are unpopular or stir up the prejudices of the social class in which the judges have for the most part been bred.

Certain of the labor cases furnish striking illustrations. For example, in the case of the *Philadelphia Cordwainers*,[64] where a group of journeymen cordwainers were tried in 1806 on an indictment for criminal conspiracy for having agreed together not to work except for higher wages, the court trying the case was unable to discover anything criminal in the object of seeking higher wages or in the means used to obtain that end. Nevertheless, at that time there prevailed among the upper classes, both in England [65]

---

[64] This, it is believed, was the first trial in America of wage-earners as such for trade-union conspiracy. The report of the case was printed as a pamphlet in 1806; it may be found reprinted in 3 COMMONS AND GILMORE, DOCUMENTARY HISTORY OF AMERICAN INDUSTRIAL SOCIETY, pp. 59–248.

[65] During this time the sentiment of the upper classes in England was so hostile to trade unions that there remained in force from 1800 to 1824 the drastic Combinations Act (40 GEO. III, c. 106), which made every journeyman workman who "enters into any combination to obtain an advance of wages or to lessen or alter the hours of work" liable to imprisonment.

In America, also, during the entire first third of the nineteenth century the crimi-

and America, a bitter feeling of hostility against the working classes; the generally accepted view was that any concerted action by the workers against their employers must be because of the very nature of things inherently criminal. One is not surprised, therefore, that in the *Philadelphia Cordwainers' Case* the defendants who had been bold enough to organize a strike for higher wages were found guilty and branded as criminals; the court was enabled to achieve the desired result by resorting to the convenient doctrine flowing from Hawkins' statement of the conspiracy law.

"A combination of workmen," said the court, "to raise their wages may be considered in a two fold point of view; one is to benefit themselves . . . the other is to injure those who do not join their society. The rule of law condemns both. . . . Hawkins, the greatest authority on the criminal law, has laid it down, that a combination to[66] maintaining one another, carrying a particular object, whether true or false, is criminal." [67]

When journeymen sought to apply the same doctrine against their employers combining to depress wages, the doctrine was flexible enough to allow the courts to exercise a very broad discretion. In the case of *Commonwealth* v. *Carlisle*,[68] decided in 1821, where journeymen sought to convict certain master shoemakers for combining to depress wages, Judge Gibson, groping for some sound principle upon which to rest the conspiracy cases, felt that a combination of employers should not be held illegal if it was formed to oppose a similar combination of employees seeking

---

nal law was the accepted method for dealing with trade unions. See early cases in 3 & 4 COMMONS & GILMORE, DOCUMENTARY HISTORY.

[66] The evident omission appears in COMMONS & GILMORE.

[67] Quoted from 3 COMMONS & GILMORE, DOCUMENTARY HISTORY OF AMERICAN INDUSTRIAL SOCIETY, p. 233. Compare the language used in the New York Hatters' Case of 1823. "Journeymen confederating and refusing to work, unless for certain wages, may be indicted for a conspiracy, . . . for this offence consists in the conspiracy and not in the refusal; and all conspiracies are illegal though the subject-matter of them may be lawful. . . Journeymen may each singly refuse to work, unless they receive an advance in wages, but if they refuse by preconcert or association they may be indicted and convicted of conspiracy. . . . The gist of a conspiracy is the unlawful confederation, and the offence is complete when the confederacy is made, and any act done in pursuit of it is no constituent part of the offence." Quoted from GROAT, AN INTRODUCTION TO THE STUDY OF ORGANIZED LABOR IN AMERICA, p. 38.

[68] Brightly's N. P. Rep. (Pa.) 36 (1821).

artificially to raise their wages; his conclusion was that "a combination to resist oppression, not merely supposed but real, would be perfectly innocent; for where the act to be done and the means of accomplishing it are lawful, and the object to be attained is meritorious, combination is not conspiracy." [69] The court finally decided that the defendants were not guilty unless they should be proved "to have been actuated by an improper motive."

It may be that these two decisions were right or it may be they were wrong; the point is that the application of the Hawkins doctrine of criminal conspiracy rendered the law applicable to labor combinations either very unpredicable or highly unjust. Since that day some of the prejudice and much of the bitterness against labor unions has passed away. The courts have in a measure corrected their mistakes; they universally to-day declare the legality and even the social necessity under modern industrial organization of trade-union associations and organized effort on the part of employees. [70] But in spite of all, there still lurks in many minds considerable of the ancient feeling; and even to-day decisions are to be found where the courts have resorted to the same vague conspiracy doctrine in order to hold criminal the members of trade unions whose concerted conduct tended in the judge's eyes to injure the social welfare, but in whose individual conduct

---

[69] Brightly's N. P. Rep. (Pa.) 42 (1821).

[70] See, for instance, the recent pronouncement of the United States Supreme Court in the case of American Steel Foundries v. The Tri-City Central Trades Council, U. S. Sup. Ct., October Term, 1921 (decision rendered Dec. 5, 1921), where Mr. Chief Justice Taft, rendering the opinion of the court, says (at page 13): "Labor unions are recognized by the Clayton Act as legal when instituted for mutual help and lawfully carrying out their legitimate objects. They have long been thus recognized by the courts. They were organized out of the necessities of the situation. A single employee was helpless in dealing with an employer. He was dependent ordinarily on his daily wage for the maintenance of himself and family. If the employer refused to pay him the wages that he thought fair, he was nevertheless unable to leave the employ and to resist arbitrary and unfair treatment. Union was essential to give laborers opportunity to deal on equality with their employer. They united to exert influence upon him and to leave him in a body in order by this inconvenience to induce him to make better terms with them. They were withholding their labor of economic value to make him pay what they thought it was worth. The right to combine for such a lawful purpose has in many years not been denied by any court. The strike became a lawful instrument in a lawful economic struggle or competition between employer and employees as to the share or division between them of the joint product of labor and capital."

the court could find nothing criminal.[71] The consequence of such decisions is that trade-union members, forced by our competitive system to fight bitter economic battles both against non-union employees and against employers intent upon driving down the price of labor, feel themselves in constant danger of being sent to jail as conspirators and criminals; and the consequent fear and sense of injustice bred by such cases has clearly not made for social peace.

Among those who depart from the historically correct doctrine that either criminal means or a criminal end must be proved to constitute a criminal conspiracy, there is, almost inevitably, the widest disagreement. Some would hold criminal a combination to commit any act *contra bonos mores* or offensive to the general moral sense of the community. Others would confine the crime of conspiracy to combinations to commit only *illegal* acts, including under "illegal" breaches of contract as well as torts; still others would confine the offense to combinations to commit torts; and a fourth group would find a crime in the case of some torts and not of others. The wideness of this disagreement itself makes for great unpredicability. If the doctrine includes combinations to commit acts *contra bonos mores*, it amounts to nothing more nor less than a device to convict defendants who concededly have violated no pre-established law whenever individual judges deem it for the interest of society so to do, — a return to justice without law. If the doctrine is confined to combinations to commit some kinds of torts but not all, there is an almost equal lack of predicability; for the courts which have suggested this have found it so impossible to draw the line between those torts which will make a combination to procure them criminal and those which will not that they have scarcely even attempted it; and utter unpredicability results. If the doctrine covers combinations to commit *all* torts, the objections based on lack of predicability lose much of their weight. But new objections arise. The result would be practically to turn every tort, planned by more than one person, into a crime. That is, the courts would be adding to the penalty worked out by the law of torts (compensation), an added criminal punishment (imprisonment) wherever more than one helped to procure the act which constitutes the tort. This would mean a

---

[71] See, for example, State *v.* Dalton, 134 Mo. App. 517, 114 S. W. 1132 (1908).

revolutionary step in the law, and one of very questionable policy, to say the least.[72] Have courts, in the entire absence of legislation, a right by judicial decision alone to take such a revolutionary step?

In spite of countless assertions in the older cases that judges find the law but do not make it, we must recognize frankly that courts do make law or legislate, and further that that is a necessary part of their judicial function. Nevertheless, one must not lose sight of the fact that judicial legislation must always differ fundamentally from legislative law making. The latter is governed purely by expediency. The legislator's only guiding principles are the economic or social or political welfare of his people. His eye must be to the future; precedents mean nothing to him. The judge, on the other hand, in making new law is not free to follow his own ideas of what would make for the social or economic welfare of the people. He is bound and restrained by established and recognized legal doctrines and principles. For instance, no matter how firmly convinced a common-law judge might be that the Anglo-American doctrine that consideration is necessary to make a promise binding is immoral and unsocial, no matter how strongly he may feel that the continental doctrine requiring no consideration for contracts would better promote the general welfare, the judge would have no right by judicial legislation to overturn at a stroke the established and well-recognized principle underlying the common law of contracts. No one has stated this better than Justice Holmes, in the case of *Stack* v. *New York, etc. Railroad*.[73]

"We agree," he says, "that, in view of the great increase of actions for personal injuries, it may be desirable that the courts should have the power in dispute. We appreciate the ease with which, if we were careless or ignorant of precedent, we might deem it enlightened to assume that power. We do not forget the continuous process of developing the law that goes on through the courts, in the form of deduction, or deny that in a clear case it might be possible even to break away from a line of decisions in favor of some rule generally admitted to be based upon

---

[72] There would seem to be little room for doubt that no court or legislature, squarely facing and comprehending the situation, would be willing to turn every tort planned by more than one, into a crime.

[73] 177 Mass. 155, 158, 58 N. E. 686 (1900).

a deeper insight into the present wants of society. But the improvements made by the courts are made, almost invariably, by very slow degrees and by very short steps. Their general duty is not to change but to work out the principles already sanctioned by the practice of the past. No one supposes that a judge is at liberty to decide with sole reference even to his strongest convictions of policy and right. His duty in general is to develop the principles which he finds, with such consistency as he may be able to attain."

Seventeen years later, speaking in the United States Supreme Court, in the case of *Southern Pacific Co.* v. *Jensen*,[74] Justice Holmes again admirably expressed the same idea.

"I recognize without hesitation," he said, "that judges do and must legislate, but they can do so only interstitially; they are confined from molar to molecular motions. A common-law judge could not say I think the doctrine of consideration a bit of historical nonsense and shall not enforce it in my court. No more could a judge exercising the limited jurisdiction of admiralty say I think well of the common-law rules of master and servant and propose to introduce them here *en bloc*."

Thus it would seem clear that even were it wise to take such a step as to turn into crimes when planned by more than one person all those acts [75] which through long-established usage have come to be held tortious but not criminal, no judge by the method of judicial legislation has the right to do so. A step of so very questionable a nature and so revolutionary and sweeping in its character must be taken, if at all, by the legislature. During the seventeenth century, when the law was undergoing a period of exceptional and vigorous growth, when morals were being largely infused into the law and many new doctrines introduced, the courts went much further in judicial legislation than to-day. Yet even the seventeenth-century judges never went so far as to lay down the doctrine that all combinations to commit torts are criminal.

Those who preach the doctrine that a conspiracy may be criminal although neither the means used nor the end pursued is criminal, resort for the most part to an argument founded upon the danger of combinations to the community. If it is the function of the

---

[74] 244 U. S. 205, 221 (1917).

[75] As is readily apparent from the context, the word "acts" here is used in its common sense of including not simply "voluntary muscular contractions," but the immediate and direct effects of such voluntary muscular contractions as well.

criminal law to protect the social welfare, they argue, whatever causes peculiar danger to the social welfare should come under the ban of the criminal law. Although a single individual's design to commit a tort is not usually criminal because not of sufficient danger to the state, yet where several combine and conspire to commit a tortious act, the increased power for wrong is so magnified, the danger to the public welfare which arises from such a nefarious plotting is so threatening, that the criminal law should be extended to cover this increased danger. As Bishop says in his *Criminal Law*,[76] adopting the words of the English Criminal Law Commissioners of 1843:

"The general principle on which the crime of conspiracy is founded is this, that the confederacy of several persons to effect any injurious object creates such a new and additional power to cause injury as requires criminal restraint; although none would be necessary were the same thing proposed, or even attempted to be done, by any person singly." [77]

Such forms of statement are very persuasive. One does not wonder that the idea has gained many adherents. Yet the danger argument is open to serious objection. The short answer to it is that if every combination to commit a tortious act does in fact so increase the danger to the state that the criminal law should undertake to prevent it, it is for the legislature, and not for the courts, to make the first move in the matter. It is always open to the legislature to declare what is so dangerous to the state that it should be branded as criminal. It is not open to the courts by sweeping judicial legislation to turn into common-law crimes every combination to commit a tortious act.

But there is another objection to the danger argument which

---

[76] 2 BISHOP, NEW CRIMINAL LAW, § 180, quoting from Seventh Rep. Crim. Law Com., 1843, p. 90.

[77] A number of judges have expressed the same idea. See, for instance, State *v.* Dalton, 134 Mo. App. 517, 535, 114 S. W. 1132 (1908), where Justice Nortoni, rendering the decision in a lower Missouri court, says: "It may be stated as a general proposition that where an additional power or enhanced ability to accomplish an injurious purpose arises by virtue of the confederation and concert of action, an element of criminal conspiracy is thereby introduced which will render sufficiently criminal either the means or the purpose otherwise merely unlawful, to sustain a conviction, although the means or the end were not such as are indictable if performed by a single individual." See also Comm. *v.* Judd, 2 Mass. 329, 337 (1807), per Parsons, C. J.; United States *v.* Lancaster, 44 Fed. 896 (1891) (per Spear, J.).

perhaps strikes still deeper. The whole argument is based essentially upon a false premise. It is based upon the sweeping generalization that the design to commit acts which are tortious or which are *contra bonos mores* is of far greater danger to the state when conceived by a combination than when conceived by a single person. But in these days of huge and powerful corporations, which form in the eyes of the law single persons, such a generalization would seem far too sweeping to accord with the actual facts of every-day life. Why should the law be such that if two steel workers plan a certain act which the law regards as tortious, they should be subject to fine and imprisonment; but if, let us say, the United States Steel Corporation plans and executes the self-same act, the criminal law should be unable to touch it? Is the danger to the state really greater in the first case than in the second? Why should a combination of individuals to commit an act which the law regards perhaps as tortious but not as criminal constitute a crime if the individuals are not incorporated, but be free from crime if they are incorporated? Is that justice? Is not the generalization upon which the danger argument is based, after all, far too hastily made and too frequently out of accord with existing facts, to furnish a sound basis for an all-important legal doctrine?

IV

So far as the state of authorities goes, apart from one outstanding exception it is exceedingly doubtful whether the majority of actual decisions, either in England or America, supports the constantly reiterated statement that to constitute a criminal conspiracy neither the object pursued nor the means used need necessarily be criminal. The fraud cases constitute the exception. They follow the doctrine which arose out of the seventeenth century development of the law of cheats. During the seventeenth and the earlier part of the eighteenth centuries the law of cheats was very unsettled; and numerous cases were prosecuted, some under individual indictments and others under indictments for conspiracy, which did not involve public frauds and which did not fall strictly under the statute of false tokens.[78] Unconsciously, these seventeenth and eighteenth century courts were greatly ex-

---

[78] 33 HEN. VIII, c. 1.

tending the law of cheats so as to make the law conform more closely to prevailing ideas of morality. When, later in the eighteenth century, the courts began to recede from their seventeenth-century pretensions, several cases were decided holding that private unfair dealings where no false token was used were not indictable in the case of individuals; [79] but in the case of conspiracies, the courts reserved their criminality. What followed was perhaps only natural. The notorious deficiencies of the criminal law of cheats provoked the judges into supplying its gaps through the method of criminal conspiracy; what really amounted to judicial legislation to cure the shortcomings of the misshapen criminal law and the silence of the legislators, was hidden behind the convenient Hawkins doctrine. The judges felt the injustice of allowing bands of manifest criminals, combining to defraud others of their property, from escaping punishment because of the criminal law's absurd deficiencies; and the result was that hard cases made bad law. In view of what has already been said the doctrine of these fraud cases, allowing conspiracy indictments where the fraud would not of itself be indictable would theoretically seem open to very serious question; but in view of the numerous decisions supporting this doctrine in cases of fraudulent representations, the fraud cases must be recognized as an acknowledged exception to the general rule. The effect of the doctrine upon modern law is in many respects very unfortunate. The law of criminal conspiracy as to fraud cases has lost well-nigh all predicability; it is almost impossible to-day to foretell whether a conspiracy conviction can be had for concerted misrepresentation or not. No one knows exactly what constitutes the fraud necessary to support such a conviction. Must it be such fraud as would be good ground for setting aside a contract? Or must it be such as would support an action for damages? Does it differ from the kind of pretense necessary to support an indictment for obtaining property by false pretenses, and if so, in just what respect? Will a mere false promise suffice? Where the purpose to cheat is plain, but the proposed deceit is such that it could not possibly actually deceive the victims, may a conspiracy indictment be had? A glance through the innumer-

---

[79] See, for instance, Rex v. Wilders, cited in 2 Burr. at 1128 (1720); Rex v. Bryan, 2 Stra. 866 (1730); Rex v. Wheatley, 2 Burr. 1125 (1761).

able fraud cases is sufficient to reveal the legal morass into which the law has strayed as a result of following in these cases the Hawkins doctrine.

Quite apart from the fraud cases, the notion gleaned from the Hawkins statement and from the leading text-writers who have been following in Hawkins' footsteps ever since, has gained the widest currency. If one were to consider all the *dicta* and unsupported statements of judges and text-writers, he would unquestionably find the very great majority in support of the doctrine that to constitute a conspiracy neither the end pursued nor the means used need necessarily be criminal. Such is the common statement, which in the words of Hobbes passes "like gaping from mouth to mouth." Yet the actual decisions, apart from the fraud cases, lend small support to the prevalent conceptions. Statements are copied from one text-book into another, and then into the encyclopædias of law; and long and formidable lists of cases are cited to support the statements. But when these lists of cases are carefully analyzed, it will be found that frequently the majority of them are cited for mere *dicta* or loose general remarks; and that of the actual decisions, not since overruled, almost all are fraud cases.

Two illustrations will suffice. Bishop in his *Criminal Law,* speaking of the crime of conspiracy, says:[80] "The unlawful thing proposed, whether as a means or an end, need not, to constitute a punishable conspiracy, be such as would be indictable if proposed or even done by a single individual." In support of this statement he cites three American and two English cases. Of the three American cases, *State* v. *Rowley,*[81] is a conspiracy to cheat and defraud and apparently fell directly within the terms of a state statute against cheating by false pretenses; *State* v. *Burnham,*[82] has been in effect apparently overruled by *State* v. *Straw;*[83] and *People* v. *Richards*[84] seems to have been also overruled by *Alderman* v. *People.*[85] The American cases cited, therefore, furnish very doubtful support for Bishop's statement. Of the two English cases cited both are conspiracies to cheat and defraud.

---

[80] 2 BISHOP, NEW CRIM. LAW, 8 ed., § 181 (1). [81] 12 Conn. 101 (1837).

[82] 15 N. H. 396 (1844). [83] 42 N. H. 393 (1861).

[84] 1 Mich. 216 (1849). [85] 4 Mich. 414, 432 (1857).

Among the more recent statements is that in the encyclopædia of law now being prepared under the name of *Corpus Juris*. Under the heading of "Conspiracy" occurs the following unqualified statement:[86] "It is not essential, however, to criminal liability that the acts contemplated should constitute a criminal offense for which, without the elements of conspiracy, one alone could be indicted." This statement is supported by so long a list of cases (with none cited *contra*) that he must be bold of heart who would venture to deny the authority back of the statement. Yet if one has the patience to analyze the decisions, case by case, as authorities for the statement quoted they fall like a house of cards. In all, thirty-seven American cases are cited. Of these, no less than ten are apparently conspiracies to commit *criminal* offenses, and therefore have no authority beyond that of mere *dicta;* seven are indictments under state statutes relating to conspiracy; three are civil actions; two have in effect been overruled by later cases within the jurisdiction; and in two the defendants were held not guilty. Sixteen of the decisions were fraud cases. When one thus analyzes the long list of authorities, he finds that, apart from the fraud cases, there are at most six or seven actual decisions supporting the statement. Of these, two were early cases for seducing or enticing away an infant girl without her father's consent, — cases which, like the fraud decisions, should perhaps be recognized as another exception to the ordinary doctrine;[87] two were in lower state courts, and should therefore hardly be regarded as authoritative, at least outside of Missouri and New Jersey, where they were decided. Of the two remaining cases, one is *State* v. *Donaldson*,[88] which was said in the later New Jersey case of *Jersey City Printing Co.* v. *Cassidy*,[89] to embody a doctrine which "may be regarded as entirely exploded,"[90] and the other was *State* v. *Bienstock*,[91] which probably should be classed among the fraud cases. "We think,

---

[86] 12 C. J. 547.

[87] Such cases seem to rest largely upon the authority of the English eighteenth-century case of Rex *v.* Delaval, 3 Burr. 1434 (1763). But, as Wright remarks (CRIMINAL CONSPIRACY, p. 32): "It can hardly be doubted that . . . the acts proposed were indictable at the date" of that case, "independently of combination, on the principle . . . that conduct grossly contrary to public morals or public decency was punishable irrespectively of combination."

[88] 32 N. J. L. 151 (1867).   [89] 63 N. J. Eq. 759, 762, 53 Atl. 230 (1902).

[90] See quotation in note 51, *supra*.   [91] 78 N. J. L. 256, 73 Atl. 530 (1909).

therefore," said the court in reaching its decision [92] "that the object of the conspiracy was unlawful, . . . and that this unlawful object was designed to be accomplished by deceit and fraud, was a cheat reaching large numbers of persons and tended to their oppression." [93]

On the following page of *Corpus Juris* the further statement is made [94] that "it will be enough if the acts contemplated are corrupt, dishonest, fraudulent, or immoral, and in that sense illegal." But five American cases and one English case are cited in support of this. Of the five American cases, the first is one where the defendants were held not guilty; the second is the decision of merely a lower state court; the third case seems to have been later overruled; the fourth was the case of a conspiracy to commit an act which was illegal; [95] and the fifth was a conspiracy to commit a criminal offense. The English case of *Rex* v. *Delaval* was a conspiracy to commit what was probably a criminal offense. [96]

These examples will suffice to show how plentiful and common are loose *dicta* scattered through the cases following the Hawkins doctrine, but how few actual decisions, apart from the fraud cases, can be actually mustered out in its support. On the other hand, decisions are not lacking which squarely decide against the Hawkins doctrine. In *Rex* v. *Turner*,[97] already discussed, Lord Ellenborough clearly rejects the doctrine; and although the decision has been criticized by some,[98] it has been followed by later cases, such as *Rex* v. *Pywell*.[99] Similar decisions are to be found among the American cases. In the case of *Commonwealth* v. *Prius*,[100] for instance, Justice Bigelow refused to convict for a conspiracy to overinsure certain goods, saying: "It was not a crime in the de-

---

[92] 78 N. J. L. 256, 274, 73 Atl. 530 (1909).

[93] One other possible decision in support of the text statement, not a fraud case, is Lanasa *v.* State, 109 Md. 602, 71 Atl. 1058 (1909). This was an indictment for a conspiracy willfully and maliciously to injure and destroy property. But in this case the evidence seems abundantly to prove the commission of acts which would be criminal quite apart from the combination or conspiracy.

[94] 12 C. J. 548.

[95] See 78 N. J. L., 256, 274, where the court says, "We think therefore that the object of the conspiracy was unlawful."

[96] See note 87, *supra*.   [97] 13 East 228 (1811).

[98] See, for instance, Lord Campbell, C. J., in Reg. *v.* Rowlands, 5 Cox 436, 490 (1851).

[99] 1 Starkie, 402 (1816).   [100] 9 Gray (Mass.) 127 (1857).

fendants to procure an over-insurance on their stock in trade. It was at most only a civil wrong. The charge of a conspiracy to do so does not therefore amount to a criminal offence."

V

In some jurisdictions special statutes have been passed to regulate the law of conspiracy; certain of these set at rest such questions as have formed the subject of the foregoing discussion. In the federal courts, for instance, the Hawkins doctrine no longer lives. The federal conspiracy statute [101] provides that

"If two or more persons conspire either to commit any offense against the United States, or to defraud the United States in any manner or for any purpose, and one or more of such parties do any act to effect the object of the conspiracy, each of the parties to such conspiracy shall be fined not more than ten thousand dollars, imprisoned not more than five years, or both."

This important statute, as is evident from its terms, follows in the main sound principles of law, and except in cases of defrauding makes impossible a federal conspiracy conviction where no federal criminal offense has been conspired. What uncertainty has arisen from the act has centered chiefly in the somewhat doubtful meaning of the words, "defraud the United States." [102] It will be noticed that the statute, unlike the common law, requires the commission of some overt act other than the mere act of conspiring.[103]

In conclusion, the fundamental similarity may be pointed out between the principles of the law of criminal and those of civil conspiracy. The one is a crime and the other a tort, and naturally, therefore, certain marked differences must exist between them.[104]

---

[101] U. S. COMP. STAT., 1918, § 10201.

[102] See 2 ZOLINE, FEDERAL CRIMINAL LAW, §§ 1038 *et seq.*

[103] In a number of states important conspiracy statutes exist, which must often be referred to in order to avoid misunderstanding the significance of decisions rendered within such states. See, for example, the New York Conspiracy statute (N. Y. PENAL LAW, § 580).

[104] The differences between criminal and civil conspiracy need not here be dwelt upon. The most striking difference is as to the necessity of some overt act. Since civil conspiracy is a tort, and since the tort remedy is compensation paid for damages suffered, no right of action exists without proof of damage; and damage comes through overt acts. In other words, unlike the law of criminal conspiracy, in civil conspiracy some overt act other than the mere conspiring must be proved. As the courts say,

Yet the fundamental principles underlying the two are essentially the same. Just as in criminal conspiracy acts not criminal when committed by individuals should not be held criminal when committed by combinations, so in civil conspiracy acts not tortious when committed by individuals should not be held tortious when committed by combinations. The mere combination cannot add illegality in the latter case any more than it can add criminality in the former. Yet, as in the criminal conspiracy cases, there is a prevalent and widespread notion abroad that in some mystical way a combination can be called a conspiracy and conspiracy lends illegality. It is only another phase of the same confusion of thought already discussed. In the case of *Lindsay and Company* v. *Montana Federation of Labor*,[105] the court squarely rejects such a doctrine in these words: [106]

"There can be found running through our legal literature many remarkable statements that an act perfectly lawful when done by one person becomes by some sort of legerdemain criminal when done by two or more persons acting in concert, and this upon the theory that the concerted action amounts to a conspiracy. But with this doctrine we do not agree. If an individual is clothed with a right when acting alone, he does not lose such right merely by acting with others, each of whom is clothed with the same right. If the act done is lawful, the combination of several persons to commit it does not render it unlawful. In other words, the mere combination of action is not an element which gives character to the act."

So, Justice Holmes, in his dissenting opinion in the case of *Vegelahn* v. *Guntner*,[107] said:

"But there is a notion which latterly has been insisted on a good deal, that a combination of persons to do what any one of them lawfully might do by himself will make the otherwise lawful conduct unlawful. It would be rash to say that some as yet unformulated truth may not be hidden under this proposition. But in the general form in which it has been presented and accepted by many courts, I think it plainly untrue, both on authority and on principle."

---

the gist of the action is the damage, and not the conspiracy. In Savile *v.* Roberts, 1 Ld. Raym. 374, 378, it was said: "An action will not lie for the greatest conspiracy imaginable, if nothing be put in execution; but if the party be damaged, the action will lie." See also Adler *v.* Fenton, 24 How. (U. S.) 407 (1860).

[105] 37 Mont. 264, 96 Pac. 127 (1908).   [106] *Ibid.*, 273.

[107] 167 Mass. 92, 107, 108, 44 N. E. 1077 (1896).

And Chief Justice Parker, rendering the opinion of the court in *National Protective Association* v. *Cumming*,[108] expressed the same idea when he said: "Whatever one man may do alone, he may do in combination with others provided they have no unlawful object in view. Mere numbers do not ordinarily affect the quality of the act." [109]

Perhaps enough has been said to make it evident that it is high time to abandon the prevalent and often repeated idea that mere combination in itself can add criminality or illegality to acts otherwise free from them. Such a doctrine grew out of an historical mistake, and has no real basis in our law. It is logically unsound and indefensible. Moreover, it is dangerous. It tends to rob the law of predicability, and to make justice depend too often upon the chance prejudices and convictions of individual judges. It has tended to make the law chaotic and formless in precisely those situations where the salvation of our troubled times most demands a precise and understandable law. Because under its cover judges are often free to legislate or to decide great social issues largely in accordance with their personal convictions, it has rendered the courts open to the bitter and constant cry of class partisanship. It is a doctrine as anomalous and provincial as it is unhappy in its results. It is utterly unknown to the Roman law; it is not found in modern Continental codes; few Continental lawyers ever heard of it. It is a fortunate circumstance that it is not encrusted so deep in our jurisprudence by past decisions of our courts that we are unable to slough it off altogether. It is a doctrine which has proved itself the evil genius of our law wherever it has touched it. May the time not be long delayed in coming when it will be nothing more than a shadow stalking through past cases, — when the Hawkins doctrine at last will be conclusively laid to rest ! *Requiescat in pace!*

Francis B. Sayre.

HARVARD LAW SCHOOL.

---

[108] 170 N. Y. 315, 63 N. E. 369 (1902).

[109] See also Bohn Mfg. Co. *v.* Hollis, 54 Minn. 223, 234, 55 N. W. 1119 (1893); Macauley Bros. *v.* Tierney, 19 R. I. 255, 264, 33 Atl. 1 (1895); Clemmitt *v.* Watson, 14 Ind. App. 38, 42 N. E. 367 (1895). Needless to say, numerous statements are also to be found holding to the contrary.

THE CONSPIRACY DILEMMA

THE CONSPIRACY DILEMMA: PROSECUTION OF GROUP CRIME OR
PROTECTION OF INDIVIDUAL DEFENDANTS. — The widespread resort by
public prosecutors to the conspiracy weapon,[1] the recent application of
the doctrine in the war crimes trials,[2] and its close relation to the prob-

---

[1] See L. Hand, J., in United States v. Falcone, 109 F.2d 579, 581 (2d Cir. 1940),
aff'd, 311 U. S. 205 (1940); O'Dougherty, *Prosecution and Defense under Conspiracy Indictments*, 9 BROOKLYN L. REV. 263 (1940).
[2] See remarks of Mr. Justice Jackson, 70 REP. N. Y. STATE BAR ASS'N 147, 154
(1947); Leventhal, Harris, Woolsey, and Farr, *The Nuernberg Verdict*, 60 HARV.
L. REV. 857, 863–81, 896–99 (1947).

lem of dealing with membership in disloyal organizations [3] has brought increasing interest in the nature and inherent dangers of the American conspiracy concept. Although the crime originated in a narrowly defined statute directed at abuses of ancient criminal procedure,[4] its expansion at an early date left no doubt about the breadth and flexibility of its application.[5] In modern times, criminal conspiracy has become the most effective, if not the only, method of reaching and punishing many forms of complex criminal organizations.[6] The elasticity of its substantive and procedural attributes has indeed made it the "darling of the modern prosecutor's nursery." [7] At the same time, however, serious dangers of abuse and oppression inhere in this elasticity. These potentialities have evoked severe criticism of the concept from judges and commentators,[8] and the necessities of effective law enforcement have frequently been found in sharp conflict with the interest of the individual defendant in securing protection from such abuses.

The Nature of the Crime. — Conspiracy is commonly defined as "a combination between two or more persons to do or accomplish a criminal or unlawful act, or to do a lawful act by criminal or unlawful means." [9] From the point of view of the individual defendant, the most serious danger arises from the criteria by which his participation in the conspiracy, and thus his individual guilt, are determined.

(a) The "Act" Element. — Liability for substantive crimes is ordi-

---

[3] See O'Brian, *Loyalty Tests and Guilt by Association*, 61 HARV. L. REV. 592, 599–605 (1948).

[4] Ordinance of Conspirators, 1304, 33 EDW. I. See Sayre, *Criminal Conspiracy*, 35 HARV. L. REV. 393, 394–96 (1922).

[5] The original expansion of the concept has been largely attributed to the Star Chamber, see, *e.g.*, 8 HOLDSWORTH, A HISTORY OF ENGLISH LAW 379, 382 (2d ed. 1937), and dates more particularly from the Poulterers Case, 9 Co. 55b, 77 Eng. Rep. 813 (K. B. 1611) (unexecuted agreement to accuse falsely is indictable). Various elements contributed to the development of the concept. Its most pronounced expansion came at a time of social unrest, and it has been suggested that it was seized upon as one device to thwart assaults upon positions of those in power. See Pollack, *Common Law Conspiracy*, 35 GEO. L. J. 328, 339 (1947). In any event, it clearly became a powerful weapon of public policy, and its expansion promptly reflected the infusion of morals into law that occurred during the seventeenth and eighteenth centuries. See Harno, *Intent in Criminal Conspiracy*, 89 U. OF PA. L. REV. 624, 626–27 (1941); Sayre, *supra* note 4, at 400.

[6] See Ritchie, *The Crime of Conspiracy*, 16 CAN. B. REV. 202 (1938).

[7] L. Hand, J., in Harrison v. United States, 7 F.2d 259, 263 (2d Cir. 1925).

[8] See, *e.g.*, *Recommendations of the Senior Circuit Judges*, REP. ATT'Y GEN. 5–6 (1925); Moscowitz, *Some Aspects of the Trial of a Criminal Case in the Federal Court*, 3 F. R. D. 380, 392 (1944); Simon, *Conspiracy — by the Prosecution*, 9 LAW SOC'Y J. 161 (1940); and notes 1 and 3 *supra*.

[9] Commonwealth v. Donoghue, 250 Ky. 343, 347, 63 S. W.2d 3, 5 (1933); *see* Pettibone v. United States, 148 U. S. 197, 203 (1893); 2 WHARTON, CRIMINAL LAW 1853 (12th ed. 1932). The crime at common law is extremely difficult to define adequately. See Pollack, *supra* note 5, at 329–32. Under the basic federal conspiracy statute, the crime is limited to combinations to commit any offense against, or to defraud, the United States. 18 U. S. C. § 371 (1948). Statutory definitions of varying breadth exist in some states. *E.g.*, IND. ANN. STAT. § 10-1101 (Burns Supp. 1947); N. J. STAT. ANN. § 2:119-1 (Supp. 1947); N. Y. PEN. LAW § 580; PA. STAT. ANN. tit. 18, § 4302 (Supp. 1947). In the absence of contrary provisions, such state statutes have been held not to eliminate common law conspiracy. State v. O'Brien, 136 N. J. L. 118, 54 A.2d 806 (Sup. Ct. 1947); *see* State v. Norton, 3 Zab. 33, 40–43 (N. J. Sup. Ct. 1850).

narily predicated upon proof of a criminal act committed in a context
of circumstance from which the requisite criminal intent may be in-
ferred.[10] In conspiracy, however, both "act" and intent are "heavily
mental in composition."[11] The agreement is the "act."[12] It constitutes
the gravamen of the offense,[13] and without it there is no conspiracy.[14]

Establishing the existence of the agreement obviously involves difficult problems of proof, most of which have been solved by a lenient attitude towards the prosecution. Since the criminal combination is frequently an organization flexible in membership, it has been held
unnecessary for the jury to find that the individual defendant was a
party to the original agreement. If he joins the conspiracy later, he
becomes equally liable with the original conspirators.[15] Even with such
an expanded view of participation, the difficulty of obtaining direct
proof that defendant has been a party to the agreement is manifest.
Persons agreeing to engage in criminal activities do not typically "go
out upon the public highways and proclaim their purpose; their meth-
ods are devious, hidden, secret and clandestine."[16] Therefore, the
courts have held that proof of a formal agreement is unnecessary to
support a finding of guilt, and that it is sufficient if the circumstances,
acts, and conduct of the parties are such as to show an agreement in
fact.[17] Such an agreement may be established by evidence that "the
parties steadily pursue the same object, whether acting separately or

---

[10] 1 BURDICK, LAW OF CRIME § 96 (1946).

[11] See Harno, *supra* note 5, at 635.

[12] See WRIGHT, THE LAW OF CRIMINAL CONSPIRACIES AND AGREEMENTS 6, 8,
50 (Carson ed. 1887). Under the federal and some state statutes, an overt act, in
addition to the mere agreement, must be shown to have been committed by the
defendant or one of his co-conspirators. *E.g.,* 18 U. S. C. § 371 (1948); CAL.
PEN. CODE § 184 (Supp. 1947); N. Y. PEN. LAW § 583. Such act need not itself
be criminal. United States v. Johnson, 165 F.2d 42 (3d Cir. 1947), *cert. denied,*
332 U. S. 852 (1948). Proof of such overt act is unnecessary under federal statutes
relating to conspiracies in restraint of trade or to monopolize, 26 STAT. 209 (1890),
15 U. S. C. §§ 1, 2 (1946), Nash v. United States, 229 U. S. 373 (1913), and conspiracies against rights of citizens secured by the Constitution or laws of the United
States. 18 U. S. C. § 241 (1948).

[13] But see Harno, *supra* note 5, at 646.

[14] Tinsley v. United States, 43 F.2d 890 (8th Cir. 1930); People v. Friedlander,
280 N. Y. 437, 21 N. E.2d 498 (1939). Thus, a single individual cannot commit the
crime of conspiracy, Evans v. People, 90 Ill. 384 (1878); and the crime has not
been committed where the agreement is merely feigned, DeLaney v. State, 164
Tenn. 432, 51 S. W.2d 485 (1932); Odneal v. State, 117 Tex. Crim. App. 97, 34
S. W.2d 595 (1931). Similarly, the crime is complete with the agreement, although the plot has not been perpetrated, WRIGHT, *op. cit. supra* note 12, at 22;
and a single agreement constitutes a single offense, however many criminal objects
are contemplated, Braverman v. United States, 317 U. S. 49 (1942).

[15] "It is immaterial when any of the parties entered the polluted stream. From
the moment he entered he is as much contaminated and held as though an original
conspirator." Coates v. United States, 59 F.2d 173, 174 (9th Cir. 1932); Commonwealth v. Anderson, 64 Pa. Super. 427 (1916); *see* People v. Mather, 4 Wend. 229,
258–61 (N. Y. 1830).

[16] Marrash v. United States, 168 Fed. 225, 229 (2d Cir. 1909).

[17] Glasser v. United States, 315 U. S. 60 (1942); Madsen v. United States, 165
F.2d 507 (10th Cir. 1947). Difficulties of proof have led to rules of evidence favor-
able to the prosecution and to leniency on the part of courts in allowing the prosecutor a wide field of operation. *See, e.g.,* People v. Fleish, 32 N. W.2d 700, 707 (Mich.

together, by common or different means, but ever leading to the same unlawful result."[18] The broad discretion vested in the jury by charges phrased in these accepted terms is extended by the rule that it is unnecessary to show that the defendant knew the full scope of the conspiracy or participated in carrying out each detail. Nor need he be acquainted with each of his alleged co-conspirators or know the exact part played by each of them.[19] Any other view would make conspiracy prosecutions impossible. Conspirators frequently do not have full knowledge of all ramifications of the combination, particularly where the organization is a complex one. Indeed, the self-interest of the conspirators would frequently demand that as few as possible have such knowledge.[20]

There are, of course, certain minimal evidentiary requirements. The accused may not be convicted merely because he is shown to have known or approved of another's proposed criminal act.[21] Evidence is required of affirmative conduct by defendant either in aid of the proposed act or indicating in some other way an agreement between the parties.[22] But except for this rule there is little consistency among the cases, and on the question of the extent of the affirmative action necessary to support a verdict of guilty, they are in direct conflict. An excellent example of this confusion is seen in the history of the treatment in the federal courts of cases involving persons who have sold articles to, or purchased from, members of a conspiracy. Proof, without more, that a defendant purchased articles of contraband from members of a conspiracy, under circumstances in which he may be presumed to have known of the illegal character of such articles, has been held insufficient to implicate the defendant.[23] For many years, however, the substantial

---

1948); Fitzgerald v. State, 188 P.2d 396, 406 (Okla. Crim. App. 1947) (evidence of collateral offenses admissible in conspiracy prosecution); O'Dougherty, *supra* note 1, at 271.

[18] United States v. Randall, 164 F.2d 284, 289 (7th Cir. 1947), *cert. denied*, 333 U. S. 856 (1948); *cf.* Lefco v. United States, 74 F.2d 66, 68 (3d Cir. 1934); People v. Cohn, 358 Ill. 326, 332, 193 N. E. 150, 153 (1934); Coleridge, J., summing up in Regina v. Murphy, 8 C. & P. 297, 310 (1837).

[19] Blumenthal v. United States, 332 U. S. 539 (1947); United States v. Manton, 107 F.2d 834 (2d Cir. 1938), *cert. denied*, 309 U. S. 664 (1940); People v. DeLano, 318 Mich. 557, 28 N. W.2d 909 (1947), *cert. denied*, 334 U. S. 818 (1948).

[20] See Note, 48 YALE L. J. 1447, 1450 (1939).

[21] Thomas v. United States, 57 F.2d 1039 (10th Cir. 1932); State v. King, 104 Iowa 727, 74 N. W. 691 (1898); *cf.* Baird v. Commonwealth, 241 Ky. 795, 45 S. W.2d 466 (1932) (no evidence of knowledge). Thus, inaction on the part of a lessor who knows that his premises are being used for unlawful purposes does not make him a party to a conspiracy. United States v. Dellaro, 99 F.2d 781 (2d Cir. 1938); Di Bonaventura v. United States, 15 F.2d 494 (4th Cir. 1926).

[22] Where knowledge is coupled with a duty to act, however, as in the case of a public officer, a conspiracy may be found on the basis of defendant's inaction. Jezewski v. United States, 13 F.2d 599 (6th Cir. 1926), *cert. denied*, 273 U. S. 735 (1926). *Contra:* People v. Kanar, 314 Mich. 242, 22 N. W.2d 359 (1946); *cf.* Burkhardt v. United States, 13 F.2d 841 (6th Cir. 1926) (no evidence of knowledge).

[23] United States v. Zeuli, 137 F.2d 845 (2d Cir. 1943); United States v. Koch, 113 F.2d 982 (2d Cir. 1940); Dickerson v. United States, 18 F.2d 887 (8th Cir. 1927). *Contra:* Wilkerson v. United States, 41 F.2d 654 (7th Cir. 1930), *cert. denied*, 282 U. S. 894 (1931).

weight of authority would impose guilt on a vendor if it were shown only that he sold to a conspirator an article essential to the success of the conspiracy and the circumstances were such that the vendor should have known of the intended illegal use.[24] In *United States v. Falcone*,[25] the Supreme Court finally reversed the latter rule and held in favor of the vendor.[26] But even in this view, little in addition to proof of sale with knowledge is required. Thus, evidence that defendant drug company, through advertising, encouraged quantity purchases of dangerous narcotics has been held sufficient to convict the company of conspiring with a physician who purchased such drugs from it and resold them to addicts.[27] In other cases, evidence that a vendor, probably to protect himself, failed to file requisite reports of the sales,[28] or made deliveries in a devious manner,[29] or made sales on credit,[30] has been held sufficient to show participation in the criminal agreement.

(b) *The Intent Element.* — The factor of intent in conspiracy is complicated by the fact that the criminal "act" is an agreement, which is itself subjective and involves as an essential element an intent to agree. To be distinguished from this intent to agree is the intent to commit some unlawful act as either the object of the agreement or the means to the attainment of that object.[31] It is the latter mental state which corresponds to the criminal intent element in other crimes.

To satisfy the requirement of criminal intent in prosecutions for ordinary common law crime, it is enough to show that the defendant performed the criminal act under circumstances in which he should reasonably have foreseen that some result unlawful in fact would follow. The intent will be implied from the doing of the act, and the fact that the defendant did not desire the particular result or that he did not know

---

[24] Borgia v. United States, 78 F.2d 550 (9th Cir. 1935), *cert. denied*, 296 U. S. 615 (1935); Zito v. United States, 64 F.2d 772 (7th Cir. 1933); *cf.* Marino v. United States, 91 F.2d 691 (9th Cir. 1937), *cert. denied sub nom.* Gullo v. United States, 302 U. S. 764 (1938); Simpson v. United States, 11 F.2d 591 (4th Cir. 1926), *cert. denied*, 271 U. S. 674 (1926). *Contra:* Young v. United States, 48 F.2d 26 (5th Cir. 1931); United States v. Russell, 41 F.2d 852 (S. D. Ala. 1930).

[25] 311 U. S. 205 (1940).

[26] Even these views, requiring evidence in addition to a showing of sale or purchase in order to establish participation by a vendor or vendee in a conspiracy, have been criticized as imposing an unwarranted restriction upon prosecutors who seek to reach all members of complicated criminal organizations. See 44 COL. L. REV. 263 (1944); 48 YALE L. J. 1447 (1939). But see 53 HARV. L. REV. 1392 (1940); 26 IOWA L. REV. 122 (1940).

[27] Direct Sales Co. v. United States, 319 U. S. 703 (1943); *cf.* United States v. Liss, 137 F.2d 995 (2d Cir. 1943), *cert. denied*, 320 U. S. 773 (1943).

[28] United States v. Pecoraro, 115 F.2d 245 (2d Cir. 1940), *cert. denied*, 312 U. S. 685 (1941).

[29] United States v. Harrison, 121 F.2d 930 (3d Cir. 1941), *cert. denied*, 314 U. S. 661 (1941).

[30] United States v. Engelsberg, 51 F.2d 479 (3d Cir. 1931), *cert. denied*, 284 U. S. 648 (1931).

[31] See Harno, *supra* note 5, at 631. It is clear that, while the two types of intent may be distinguished for analytical purposes, from a psychological point of view such a separation may be less valid. *Cf. ibid.* Recognition of this fact may account to some extent for the failure of the courts to apply the distinction in practice. See p. 281 *infra.*

it was unlawful is no defense.[32] Where the charge is conspiracy, it is often said that proof is required not merely that the defendant intended to do an act, as the object of the combination, forbidden by law, but that he intended to do an act which he knew to be unlawful; and this requirement is not satisfied by mere proof of the agreement or even of its execution, at least where the object was merely *malum prohibitum*.[33] Since the proof of such specific knowledge and intent is obviously difficult, this requirement would seem to impose a severe limitation upon the scope of the conspiracy concept. But in practice, doubtless due in some measure to the pressure of these evidentiary difficulties, the rule has frequently been rejected, ignored, or loosely applied.[34] This laxity may also be attributable in part to decisions in cases involving conspiracies in restraint of trade under the Sherman Act [35] or similar statutes. Such enactments are aimed primarily at removing certain economic ills. In imposing liability under the statutes, therefore, the courts have, not illogically, tended to stress the presence of the proscribed activities rather than the nature of the intent with which they were undertaken, or of the agreement itself. Thus, it has been held that by purposely engaging in a combination which will operate in fact to restrain trade, the defendants become chargeable with intending that result and that allegation and proof of a specific intent to restrain trade are unnecessary.[36] Without recognizing that the remedial nature of such statutes inevitably has affected decisions thereunder, courts have some-

---

[32] 1 BURDICK, LAW OF CRIME §§ 112-13 (1946); MILLER, HANDBOOK OF CRIMINAL LAW § 16 (1934); Note, 38 HARV. L. REV. 96 (1924).
[33] Landen v. United States, 299 Fed. 75 (6th Cir. 1924); Commonwealth v. Benesch, 290 Mass. 125, 194 N. E. 905 (1935); People v. Powell, 63 N. Y. 88 (1875); see Harno, *supra* note 5, at 635-45.
[34] Chadwick v. United States, 141 Fed. 225 (6th Cir. 1905) (rule rejected); People v. Cohn, 358 Ill. 326, 193 N. E. 150 (1934) (rule ignored); Cruz v. United States, 106 F.2d 828 (10th Cir. 1939) (general corrupt motive sufficient); *cf.* Keegan v. United States, 325 U. S. 478, 506 (1945) (dissenting opinion); United States v. Mack, 112 F.2d 290, 292 (2d Cir. 1940). It ought to be enough, in any event, that the object is so obviously antisocial that it should reasonably have been known to be unlawful. *See* Mitchell v. State, 248 Ala. 169, 172, 27 So.2d 36, 38 (1946); Note, 38 HARV. L. REV. 96, 97 (1924).
[35] 26 STAT. 209 (1890), 15 U. S. C. § 1 (1946).
[36] United States v. Patten, 226 U. S. 525 (1913); United States v. General Motors Corp., 121 F.2d 376 (7th Cir. 1941), *cert. denied*, 314 U. S. 618 (1941); *cf.* Appalachian Coals, Inc. v. United States, 288 U. S. 344 (1933). "To require a greater showing would cripple the Act." United States v. Griffith, 334 U. S. 100, 105 (1948). The courts have been equally liberal in finding the element of agreement from the conduct of the parties in such cases. *E.g.*, United States v. Masonite Corp., 316 U. S. 265 (1942) (competing licensees entered into similar contracts with patent owner); Interstate Circuit, Inc. v. United States, 306 U. S. 208 (1939) (competing movie distributors entered into similar contracts with important theater chain); see Adelman, *Effective Competition and the Antitrust Laws*, 61 HARV. L. REV. 1289, 1324-27 (1948). The Sherman Act has been called "a carefully studied attempt to bring within the Act every person engaged in business whose activities might restrain or monopolize commercial intercourse among the states. That Congress desired to go to the utmost extent of its constitutional power in preventing restraints of trade and attempts to monopolize . . . appears very clear." United States v. New York Great Atlantic & Pacific Tea Co., 67 F. Supp. 626, 677 (E. D. Ill. 1946).

times on the authority of such decisions held proof of specific intent unnecessary in other types of conspiracy cases.[37]

Other Aspects of Prosecution and Punishment. — Almost from its inception, the conspiracy prosecution involves procedural elements, to some extent necessary consequences of the inherent nature of the crime, which may prove prejudicial to the defendant. Thus, without violation of the Sixth Amendment,[38] venue may be laid as to any or all of the conspirators in any place where an act was done by any of them in furtherance of the common design.[39] The danger of abuse, in that defendant may be taken for trial to a place where he has never been, is clear.[40] Yet the frequent difficulty of proving the place where the agreement itself was in fact entered into would often make conspiracy prosecutions impossible if venue were limited to the place of agreement.[41] Additional possibilities for abuse are inherent in the practice of trying large numbers of defendants together in the name of expediency and economy,[42] but at the expense of possible confusion on the part of the jury and of unwarranted imputation of guilt.[43]

The consequences of proving defendant's participation in the conspiracy are also serious. The acts and declarations of his co-conspirators in furtherance of the conspiracy become admissible against him,[44] and he becomes equally liable for those acts.[45] He is guilty on the conspiracy

---

[37] *E.g.*, Hamburg-American Steam Packet Co. v. United States, 250 Fed. 747 (2d Cir. 1918), *cert. denied*, 246 U. S. 662 (1918); State v. Kemp, 126 Conn. 60, 9 A.2d 63 (1939), both relying on United States v. Patten, *supra* note 36.

[38] "In all criminal prosecutions, the accused shall enjoy the right to a speedy and public trial, by an impartial jury of the State and district wherein the crime shall have been committed . . . ."

[39] Hyde v. United States, 225 U. S. 347 (1912); Rex v. Brisac, 4 East 164, 102 Eng. Rep. 792 (K. B. 1803); *see* People v. Mather, 4 Wend. 229, 259 (N. Y. 1830).

[40] See Justice Holmes, dissenting in Hyde v. United States, *supra* note 39, at 386–87.

[41] *Id.* at 363 (majority opinion).

[42] In Allen v. United States, 4 F.2d 688 (7th Cir. 1925), *cert. denied sub nom.* Hunter v. United States, 267 U. S. 597 (1925); Mullen v. United States, 267 U. S. 598 (1925); Johnson v. United States, 268 U. S. 689 (1925), it was held that the mere fact that the prosecution proceeded to trial with 75 defendants did not constitute reversible error. Such a large number of defendants is not unusual. See O'Dougherty, *supra* note 1, at 270.

[43] *See* Kotteakos v. United States, 328 U. S. 750, 772–74, 776–77 (1946). Also see the prejudicial circumstances described in United States v. Central Supply Ass'n, 6 F. R. D. 526, 533–35 (N. D. Ohio 1947). *But see* United States v. Liss, 137 F.2d 995, 999 (2d Cir. 1943), *cert. denied*, 320 U. S. 773 (1943): ". . . if we are to clutch at such shadows, the criminal prosecution of complicated crime becomes impossible, and the phantom of the innocent man convicted will prevent any effective enforcement of the law." United States v. Cohen, 145 F.2d 82, 95 (2d Cir. 1944), *cert. denied*, 323 U. S. 799 (1945); see Note, 48 YALE L. J. 1447 (1939).

[44] See 2 WHARTON, EVIDENCE IN CRIMINAL CASES § 699 (11th ed. 1935). Such evidence becomes admissible although the prosecution is for the substantive crime and not for the conspiracy. People v. Luciano, 277 N. Y. 348, 14 N. E.2d 433 (1938). The acts or declarations must, of course, have occurred before termination of the conspiracy. Fiswick v. United States, 329 U. S. 211 (1946).

[45] Pinkerton v. United States, 328 U. S. 640 (1946); State v. Williams, 356 Mo. 1048, 204 S. W.2d 748 (1947). But see 16 FORD. L. REV. 275 (1947); 56 YALE L. J. 371 (1947).

charge although he proves subsequent withdrawal, since the crime is complete with the agreement.[46] Finally, the punishment imposed for the conspiracy may be considerably greater than that imposed for commission of the substantive crime that was the object of the conspiracy.[47]

Function of the Conspiracy Concept. — Several factors, seldom articulated by the courts, seem to underlie this concept of the unique criminality of group action.[48] Basic is the increased danger to the public welfare and safety that exists in the combination of united wills to effect a harmful object, as contrasted with the menace of the criminal purpose of a single individual.[49] Reliance on the co-operation of co-conspirators and the intent to support and aid them in the future increases the likelihood of criminal conduct on the part of individual conspirators.[50] And it is more difficult to guard against the antisocial designs of a group of persons than those of an individual.[51] Thus, the crucial importance of the conspiracy weapon stems from its effectiveness in reaching organized crime. The advantages of division of labor

---

[46] Dill v. State, 35 Tex. Crim. App. 240, 33 S. W. 126 (1895). Where an overt act is required by statute before the crime is indictable, withdrawal before such overt act is a defense. *See* United States v. Britton, 108 U. S. 199, 204–05 (1883). Proof of withdrawal will avoid liability for subsequent substantive crimes committed by former co-conspirators, Pinkard v. State, 30 Ga. 757 (1860), but once proved, the conspiracy is presumed to continue until the defendant makes some affirmative act of withdrawal. Hyde v. United States, 225 U. S. 347 (1912); Miller v. United States, 277 Fed. 721 (4th Cir. 1921). Courts have imposed severe requirements with regard to proof of such withdrawal. *E.g.,* Eldredge v. United States, 62 F.2d 449 (10th Cir. 1932); Commonwealth v. Doris, 287 Pa. 547, 135 Atl. 313 (1926); *see* State v. Allen, 47 Conn. 121, 139 (1879).

[47] United States v. Stevenson, 215 U. S. 200 (1909); Clune v. United States, 159 U. S. 590 (1895). Illustrating the disparity in punishment that may be available, *see* Fisher v. United States, 2 F.2d 843, 847 (4th Cir. 1924) (dissenting opinion), *cert. denied,* 266 U. S. 629 (1924); State v. Setter, 57 Conn. 461, 18 Atl. 782 (1889).

[48] A conspiracy may be criminal although the proposed purpose would not be criminal in an individual. *E.g.,* State v. Parker, 114 Conn. 354, 158 Atl. 797 (1932); Smith v. People, 25 Ill. 17 (1860); State v. Continental Purchasing Co., 119 N. J. L. 257, 195 Atl. 827 (Sup. Ct. 1938), *aff'd per curiam,* 121 N. J. L. 76, 1 A.2d 377 (1938); *cf.* United States v. Winner, 28 F.2d 295 (N. D. Ill. 1928), *aff'd,* 33 F.2d 507 (7th Cir. 1929) (conspiracy to commit an offense which is punishable only in an action by private informer to recover penalty). And, of course, where the object is one criminal in an individual, the conspiracy is punishable even before it reaches the point where it would be indictable in an individual as an attempt. See Justice Holmes, dissenting in Hyde v. United States, 225 U. S. 347, 387–88 (1912).

[49] *See* Commonwealth *ex rel.* Chew v. Carlisle, 1 Brightly 36, 41 (Pa. N. P. 1821); 2 BISHOP, CRIMINAL LAW § 180 (9th ed. 1923); Holdsworth, *Conspiracy and Abuse of Legal Process,* 37 L. Q. REV. 462, 467 (1921).

[50] *See* State v. Dalton, 134 Mo. App. 517, 537, 114 S. W. 1132, 1139 (1908); Note, 37 HARV. L. REV. 1121, 1123 (1924). And *see* United States v. Rabinowich, 238 U. S. 78, 88 (1915); United States v. Lancaster, 44 Fed. 896, 899 (C. C. W. D. Ga. 1891), both suggesting the adverse effect of the conspiracy on the law-abiding character of individual participants.

[51] *See* State v. Buchanan, 5 Harris & J. 317, 354 (Md. 1821); Commonwealth v. Judd, 2 Mass. 329, 337 (1807). The best illustration is the conspiracy to defraud. A voucher of reliability and honesty given by a supposedly independent third person will almost invariably instill a feeling of confidence in the victim which the principal perpetrator of the fraud could rarely achieve alone. See, *e.g.,* People v. Daniels, 192 P.2d 788 (Cal. App. 1948).

and complex organization characteristic of modern economic society have their counterparts in many forms of criminal activity.[52] Manufacture or importation and distribution of contraband goods, for example, often demands a complicated organization. The interrelations of the parties in schemes to defraud may be highly complex. Except for the conspiracy device, society would be without protection until the criminal object is actually executed or at least sufficiently approached to become indictable as an attempt; and even then often only the actual perpetrator and perhaps his immediate accessories could be reached. Through the conspiracy dragnet, all participants in gang operations, the catspaw and his principal, those who contribute from afar as well as the immediate actors, can be punished, often before the evil design has fully matured into the criminal act.[53] To accomplish this result, however, the jury must be permitted to draw broad inferences of the agreement and intent from evidence of an amorphous context of acts, circumstances, and conduct. The danger necessarily follows that the defendant "might be found in the net of a conspiracy by reason of the relation of [his] acts to acts of others, the significance of which [he] may not have appreciated." [54]

Measures for Safeguarding the Defendant. — The dangers inherent in conspiracy prosecutions have been widely recognized, and diverse safeguards have been proposed. Pleas to the self-restraint of prosecutors have sometimes been made, but these, even from the most authoritative sources, cannot, in light of experience, be hoped to evoke much in the way of a satisfactory response.[55] Other critics have appealed for a more liberal use of the discretion of the trial judge to compel severances.[56] It has been further suggested that in charging juries, courts should stress the need for finding an actual agreement, rather than emphasize the lack of necessity of a formal or verbal agreement and the possibility of tacit consent and purely circumstantial proof.[57] Careful distinction between the intent necessary for the agreement and the specific intent to do an unlawful act, and an explicit requirement that each be shown, has been proposed as another means of lessening the peril.[58] But although such practices, by imposing more stringent evidentiary requirements, mitigate to some extent the dangers involved, the wholesale application of

---

[52] See Kauffman, *Joinder of Conspiracy and Attempt*, 28 GEO. L. J. 608, 613 (1940).

[53] See Harno, *supra* note 5, at 645–46; Ritchie, *supra* note 6; 27 J. CRIM. L. 128, 130 (1936).

[54] Mr. Justice Frankfurter, concurring in Von Moltke v. Gillies, 332 U. S. 708, 728 (1948).

[55] Compare United States v. Kissel, 173 Fed. 823, 828 (C. C. S. D. N. Y. 1909), *rev'd on other grounds*, 218 U. S. 601 (1910), and *Recommendations of the Senior Circuit Judges*, REP. ATT'Y GEN. 5–6 (1925), with United States v. Falcone, 109 F.2d 579, 581 (2d Cir. 1940), *aff'd*, 311 U. S. 205 (1940).

[56] See Frank, J., dissenting in United States v. Liss, 137 F.2d 995, 1004 (2d Cir. 1943), *cert. denied*, 320 U. S. 773 (1943); *cf.* United States v. Central Supply Ass'n, 6 F. R. D. 526 (N. D. Ohio 1947).

[57] See Cousens, *Agreement as an Element in Conspiracy*, 23 VA. L. REV. 898, 910 (1937).

[58] See Harno, *supra* note 5, at 646–47.

these measures to protect the defendant is impossible in view of the
function served by the conspiracy concept and the reasons for its peculiar vitality.

Since these solutions have proved unavailing, it appears that the only
recourse — if a satisfactory compromise between defendants' interests
and the needs of prosecutors is to be achieved — is a careful limitation,
in the light of the reasons for outlawing conspiracies, of the types of
agreement made criminally punishable. Such an approach, while it
would not avoid the dangers inherent in conspiracy prosecutions, would
limit the incidence of the device and thus reduce the number of defendants who are exposed to those dangers. As has been suggested, conspiracies are made criminal because of the increased likelihood, as a result of the agreement, that antisocial acts will be committed, and
committed successfully. If this view is correct, an agreement should be
punishable only (1) where it greatly increases such likelihood, or (2)
where the object — the means or end — contemplated is of such an
extremely serious nature that even a slight increase in the probability
of successful execution should be punished. The determination of what
objects fall within such categories is properly a legislative function.
Conceding that conspiracies to commit serious crimes should be punished, the concept of conspiracy as now defined, proscribing conspiracies to commit *any* unlawful act, seems considerably overexpanded. Particularly in punishing conspiracies to commit acts which themselves are
not criminal,[59] the outlines of the present law seem unduly broad. Since
the danger is that antisocial acts will be successfully committed, if the
acts themselves are not of such serious nature as to be punishable, the
conspiracy to commit them should not generally be so.[60] Moreover, in
the case of conspiracies to commit many minor criminal offenses, in
which a lone wolf may operate as effectively as a complex organization,
the conspiracy concept seems inapplicable.[61] The peculiar value of the
concept lies in such fields as traffic in stolen goods and narcotics, coun-
terfeiting, schemes to defraud and to evade certain taxes and duties,

---

[59] See, *e.g.*, cases cited note 48 *supra*.

[60] See Sayre, *supra* note 4; 2 WHARTON, CRIMINAL LAW §§ 1603, 1629 (12th
ed. 1932), criticizing the doctrine in its application to objects not indictable in
individuals, because of the uncertainty thereby introduced into the law, and on
other grounds. These commentators suggest limiting the concept to conspiracies
to commit criminal objects, with the possible addition of conspiracies to commit
certain frauds not otherwise indictable. See also WRIGHT, *op. cit. supra* note 12,
at 66–67. The broad statutory definitions of conspiracy in some states seem
equally undesirable. Under the federal statute, of course, this problem of conspiracies to commit noncriminal acts is not present. *See* Gebardi v. United States,
287 U. S. 112, 120 n.4 (1932); note 9 *supra*. But see 77 U. OF PA. L. REV. 535
(1929); note 48 *supra*.

[61] ". . . on the whole it is conceived that there can be very few kinds of minor
offences, the quality of which can be so altered by agreement as to make it
necessary to punish them by indictment; and that those kinds ought to be considered beforehand by the legislature and specified in the written law." WRIGHT,
op. cit. supra note 12, at 66. Thus, even the federal statute, limiting the concept
to conspiracies to commit "offenses against the United States" seems unduly broad.
See note 9 *supra*.

where the fact of combination may add greatly to the effective perpetration of the offense.[62]

At the same time that legislatures are re-examining the outlines of the crime to determine what agreements fall within the aforementioned categories,[63] they should also reconsider the punishment imposed for conspiracy. Since the basis for making conspiracy a crime is the increased danger that certain acts will be done, the punishment for the former should rarely be greater than it would be if the defendant were being prosecuted for committing the acts themselves.[64] A step in this direction has been taken in the new Federal Criminal Code, which, although increasing the possible punishment for conspiracies generally, provides that where the object of the conspiracy is a misdemeanor, the punishment shall not exceed that for the substantive offense.[65] A more rational correlation between the punishment for conspiracy and that for the substantive crime that is its object would reduce one incentive for prosecutors to choose the former device where conviction for the substantive crime might be obtained.

---

[62] See Waddill, J., dissenting in Fisher v. United States, 2 F.2d 843, 847 (4th Cir. 1924), cert. denied, 266 U. S. 629 (1924).

[63] See the intimation of the Senior Circuit Judges directed at Congress in REP. ATT'Y GEN. 6 (1925).

[64] But see United States v. Rabinowich, 238 U. S. 78, 88 (1915).

[65] 18 U. S. C. § 371 (1948). "Such a punishment would seem as desirable for all conspiracies . . . [but] because of the strong objections of prosecutors . . . the revised section represents the best compromise that could be devised between sharply conflicting views." Reviser's Notes to § 371, 18 U. S. C. 2476 (1948).

THE LOGIC OF CONSPIRACY

THE LOGIC OF CONSPIRACY—United States v. Spock, 416 F.2d 165 (1969). The Court of Appeals of the First Circuit in *United States v. Spock* reversed the conspiracy convictions of the four defendants—Dr. Benjamin Spock, Rev. William Sloane Coffin, Mitchell Goodman, and Michael Ferber—for aiding and abetting registrants to evade the military draft. However, Goodman and Coffin were remanded to the district court for a new trial. The decision is the most recent delineation of the elements requisite to a conspiracy. These elements provide the outer limits for a doctrine, the history of which exemplifies the "tendency of a principle to expand itself to the limits of its logic."[1] It is the purpose of this note to consider the doctrine of conspiracy, to delineate the approach adopted by the court in *United States v. Spock*, and to ask if the court's interpretation exceeded the limits of the logic of conspiracy.

I. LOGIC OF CONSPIRACY

A definition of conspiracy is helpful in orienting a discussion of the doctrine. Perkins has formulated the broadest definition: "[a] conspiracy is a combination for an unlawful purpose."[2] Beyond an introduction, definitions lose their value, because the elements of a conspiracy vary with the logic supporting them. Since the elements compose the concept being defined, it is inappropriate to begin with a restrictive definition.

The traditional assumption underlying conspiracy prosecution is that there is an increased danger to society in collective action:[3] the possibility of abandonment of the scheme is reduced by reliance on the cooperation of coconspirators, its execution is more likely to succeed with ready replacements, and the magnitude of

---

[1] B. CARDOZO, THE NATURE OF THE JUDICIAL PROCESS 51 (1921). This phrase was applied to the doctrine of conspiracy by Justice Jackson in a concurring opinion in Krulewitch v. United States, 336 U.S. 440, 445 (1949).

[2] R. PERKINS, CRIMINAL LAW 529 (1957) [hereinafter cited as PERKINS]. The most common judicial definition appears in Pettibone v. United States, 148 U.S. 197, 203 (1893):

> A conspiracy is sufficiently described as a combination of two or more persons, by concerted action, to accomplish a criminal or unlawful purpose, or some purpose not in itself criminal or unlawful, by criminal or unlawful means . . . .

Perkins, finding the phrasing repetitious, produced the more terse definition. Holmes' reference to conspiracy as a "partnership in criminal purposes," Pinkerton v. United States, 328 U.S. 640, 644 (1946), is often adopted in popular discussion. See, e.g., Orton v. United States, 221 F. 2d 632, 633 (4th Cir. 1955).

[3] *Developments in the Law—Criminal Conspiracy*, 72 HARV. L. REV. 923 (1959). The authors refer to the "specified object" rationale which focuses on the objects specifically contemplated by the conspiracy, and the "general danger" rationale which looks to the dangers inherent in the grouping. *Id.* at 925. The latter is more relevant to the underlying logic of conspiracy, for the former is a concern in the commission or planning of all crimes.

the potential harm may be proportional to the number of persons involved.[4] Once effectively organized, the grouping may serve as a focus for further unlawful activity.[5] Since the unlawful combination is seen as posing greater danger to society than individual criminal conduct, its members are subjected to punishment for collective involvement rather than specific action.[6]

The logic of conspiracy varies with the nature of the elements on which the concept is based. When the additional danger to society of collective action is considered the underlying rationale for prosecuting individuals as a conspiracy,[7] two elements form the basis of the conspiracy—(a) relationship among individuals sufficient to produce collective action, and (b) an unlawful purpose, such that the dimension added is danger.[8]

The continuum of possible interpretations of conspiracy moves from the broadest formulation of the requisite elements, applicable to all instances of alleged conspiracy, to a narrower concept of conspiracy which distinguishes instances in which first amendment rights are involved:

> *Form a.* Any *agreement*, for the full range of unlawful purposes, is a relationship sufficient to present the added danger of collective action.

---

[4] R. PERKINS 535. *See also* People v. Comstock, 147 Cal. App. 2d 287, 305 P.2d 228 (1956); Woods v. United States, 240 F.2d 37 (D.C. Cir. 1957).

[5] *Criminal Conspiracy, supra* note 3, at 925. *See also* United States v. Rabinowich, 238 U.S. 78, 88 (1915). As Judge Coffin summarized in his dissent to *United States v. Spock:*

> [T]he core idea underlying the conspiracy theory is that disciplined, concerted action poses a greater threat to society than does individual or uncoordinated group effort in that larger numbers permit a division of labor, and discipline makes withdrawal from the enterprise less likely.

416 F.2d at 184.

[6] R. PERKINS 535. Perkins discusses some instances where unlawful combinations do not have any element of added danger, *i.e.*, when the substantive offense requires concerted action and none participate but the necessary parties.

[7] *Criminal Conspiracy, supra* note 3, at 983. The author adds that in practical rather than logical terms, the rationale behind conspiracy may be solely the evidentiary and jurisdictional advantages. The more appealing of these advantages were listed in *Tea-party Theory of Conspiracy,* 44 MARQ. L. REV. 73 (1960): (1) quantum of proof frequently less; (2) statute of limitations for the substantive offense extended by charge of continuing conspiracy; and (3) coconspirator exception to the hearsay rule. While this practical rationale must be recognized, it is a result of the rules which have developed governing conspiracy prosecution rather than part of the logic of the doctrine itself.

[8] A third element, individual adherence to the illegality, is discussed in *Spock,* 416 F.2d at 176-80. Analytically, this element, rather than being essential to the creation of the conspiracy, is used as a check to assure that each member of a group is committed to the unlawful purpose posited as element b. That added element is especially crucial when the organization has mixed legal and illegal ends, as in Scales v. United States, 367 U.S. 203 (1961).

Form b. Any *combination,* for the full range of unlawful purposes, is a relationship sufficient to present the added danger of collective action.

Form c. Any combination, for the full range of unlawful purposes, is a relationship sufficient to present the added danger of collective action; but members of a combination who submit their opposition to current definitions of unlawful conduct to the marketplace of ideas may reduce their potential for added danger. To the extent that the potential is decreased, a less restrictive alternative should be employed.

Form d. Any combination, for the full range of unlawful purposes, other than those which submit their opposition to current definitions of unlawful conduct to the marketplace of ideas, results in added danger to society.

This continuum is not intended to exhaust the possible formulations applicable to conspiracy. Nor does it offer any judgment as to which of the formulations is preferable. It does, however, outline distinctions which are relevant and underline the problems which any court considering a conspiracy charge must resolve.

The threshold requirement for a conspiracy is the relationship among members of the alleged conspiracy. If a relationship sufficient to cross this threshold is not established, no conspiracy exists. *Form a* refers to this relationship as an agreement, *form b* as a combination. The distinction is more than one of semantics; it is a matter of logical sufficiency.[9] Agreement has a broad scope which can reach from parallel responses in thought or action to a common concern, through a shifting cluster of individuals sharing some ideas, to a cohesive organization with explicit goals. The unity of idea or purpose, the meeting of the minds in contract terms, is necessary to a conspiracy. Proponents of *form a* would find this unity sufficient to constitute a conspiracy as well.[10]

Proponents of *form b,* while admitting that an agreement comprises a necessary condition, find only an actual combination sufficient to yield a conspiracy.[11] A combination, in contrast, is the product of an agreement, and connotes an intent to come together

---

[9] A *necessary* condition is a condition which must be met, but which may not, of itself, produce the result. A *sufficient* condition, when met, produces the result.

[10] *See, e.g.,* United States v. Falcone, 311 U.S. 205, 210 (1940):
The gist of the offense of conspiracy as defined by sec. 37 of the Criminal Code, 18 USCA § 88, is agreement among the conspirators to commit an offense attended by an act of one or more of the conspirators to effect the object of the conspiracy.

[11] R. Perkins 530. Perkins, who supports the proposition that the conspiracy is the resulting combination, still sees a meeting of the minds, i.e., a unity of design and purpose, as necessary to the conspiracy. *See also* Krulewitch v. United States, 336 U.S. 440, 447-8 (1949) (Jackson, J., concurring); People v. Campbell, 132 Cal. App. 2d 262, 281 P.2d 912 (1955).

regarding the subject of agreement, whether or not action follows.[12]
Since a combination is the result of the agreement,[13] the agreement still is necessary. The sufficiency of agreement, therefore,
is the issue which distinguishes *forms a* and *b.*

Both approaches are found in court decisions, though judges frequently are unclear in their opinions which formulation they are
adopting. The practical effect of the distinction is reflected in the
type and amount of proof required. As a minimum, parallelism of
thought or reaction is sufficient to establish agreement. A combining, or coming together in idea or act, negates any reliance on
parallelism and forces the prosecution into an area infinitely more
difficult of proof.[14]

The distinction between agreement and combination turns on a
question of logical sufficiency. The emphasis of *forms c* and *d,* or
the effect of using first amendment rights to submit opposition to
definitions of unlawful conduct to the marketplace of ideas, is
rather a matter of emotional or political orientation. These forms
involve the extent to which one sees society threatened or en-
dangered by certain conduct or expression.[15] The range of judicial response runs from consistent application of *form a* or *form
b* without reference to these added variables, through a feeling
that such variables may reduce potential danger and thus call for
extra protection, to an assertion that the involvement of first amendment dissent per se negates added danger and compels the highest
protection.

Once beyond the point where it is recognized that cases involving
first amendment rights of speech and association used to oppose
definitions of unlawful conduct are distinguishable, the line is
clearly drawn between those who will recognize that these cases

---

12 *See* Fraina v. United States, 255 F. 28 (2d Cir. 1918): "The essence
of a conspiracy is the combination, and the act of combining should
ordinarily be first made to appear, before proving the acts and declarations
of the co-conspirators." *Id.* at 34.

13 Perkins explains most succinctly:
  Since the conspiracy is the combination resulting from the agreement,
  rather than the mere agreement itself it follows that the verb conspire where used in law, has reference to the formation of the combination. "To conspire" means "to combine" and not merely "to
  agree."
PERKINS 530. The agreement alone is insufficient: "The essence of the
crime is the unlawful combination." *Id.* at 565.

14 It is precisely this difficulty of proof which has given rise to
special rules of evidence which allow a freer use of inference and circumstance. *See, e.g.,* Glasser v. United States, 315 U.S. 60, 80 (1942).
  "The evidence of conspiracy is largely circumstantial, but . . . the
nature of a conspiracy is such that it can rarely be proved any other way."
White v. United States, 394 F.2d 49, 51 (1968).

15 This danger or threat is the second of the two elements discussed
as constituting the basis of a conspiracy. *See* text accompanying note 8,
supra.

may deserve a higher standard of protection, and those who find such protection compelled. Proponents of a less restrictive alternative usually will recognize that openness of dissent towards definitions of crime reduces the threat of a conspiracy to society, because the dissent can be countered by the government's arguments, and the occurrence of the substantive crime can be closely anticipated.[16] Advocates of this position require application of the least restrictive alternative only to the extent that the potential danger is reduced. Individual prosecution for the substantive offense is the most obvious less restrictive alternative, for it does not inhibit collective implementation of first amendment rights of speech and assembly. Though an infringement of rights of speech and assembly may appear in the prosecution of a single person for the substantive offense, the direct burden is limited to the accused. If members of a group identify closely with the individual prosecuted, the indirect infringement on rights of speech and assembly may be as great as the effect of a conspiracy prosecution.

Form d recognizes that the implementation of overt association and public expression within the first amendment guarantee may well be the preferred basis of a democratic society. As depicted in Wallace Mendelson's analysis,

> Democracy, then, is the *unfettered exchange of ideas* with public control of *action* in accordance with those thoughts which win acceptance in the marketplace of reason.[17]

This conclusion may be based on the belief that such an exchange is the best test of truth. Mr. Justice Holmes expressed that faith.

> But when men have realized that time has upset many fighting faiths, they may come to believe even more than they believe the very foundations of their own conduct that the ultimate good desired is better reached by free trade in ideas—that the best test of truth is the power of the thought to get itself accepted in the competition of the market, and that truth is the only ground upon which their wishes safely can be carried out.[18]

The Supreme Court of the United States recently reiterated this value in *New York Times v. Sullivan* when it pronounced a "profound national commitment to the principle that debate on public issues should be uninhibited, robust and wide-open . . . ."[19]

---

[16] *See* U.S. v. Robe, 389 U.S. 258, 265-68 (1967); Aptheker v. Secretary of State, 378 U.S. 500, 512-14 (1964); Shelton v. Tucker, 364 U.S. 479, 488-89 (1960); Krulewitch v. United States, 336 U.S. 440, 457 (1949) (Jackson, J., concurring).
[17] W. MENDELSON, JUSTICES BLACK AND FRANKFURTER: CONFLICT IN THE COURT 52 (2d ed. 1966).
[18] Abrams v. United States, 250 U.S. 616, 630 (1919) (Holmes & Brandeis, JJ., dissenting).
[19] 376 U.S. 254, 270 (1964). Although the suit was for libel, the case involved political criticism and may, therefore, be analogous to a conspiracy prosecution for acts or words of dissent.

As a basis of democracy and a test of truth, the implementation of freedom of expression offers society an added value, early recognized by Cato:

> Without freedom of thought there can be no such thing as wisdom; and no such thing as publick (sic) liberty, without freedom of speech . . . .[20]

Finding an added value to society in such a conspiracy, rather than an added danger, the reason for applying the doctrine of conspiracy is not present and first amendment protection is compelled.[21]

The continuum of formulations provides a framework for an analysis of the opinion in *Spock* and an opportunity to determine whether the logic adopted by the court prohibited it from considering the relevant elements of the alleged conspiracy.

II.   UNITED STATES v. SPOCK: THE DECISION

Benjamin Spock, Michael Ferber, Mitchell Goodman, and William Sloane Coffin were convicted under a single indictment for conspiracy in violation of the Military Selective Service Act of 1967[22] and sentenced to two years imprisonment with varying fines. In essence it was charged that they conspired to "counsel, aid and abet" young men to avoid the military draft.

The basis of their actions was opposition to United States involvement in the war in Vietnam. The chronology of their individual actions encompassed the drafting and signing of the *Call to Resist Illegitimate Authority*,[23] the press conference publicizing the *Call*,[24]

---

[20] Cato, *Letters*, quoted in M. SUMMERS, FREE SPEECH AND POLITICAL PROTEST vii (1967).

[21] Judge Coffin in his dissent in *Spock*, 416 F.2d at 185, is tempted to agree, but refuses:

> One is tempted to say the law should recognize no overt conspiracy in the sensitive area of public discussion and opinion. But this would be to go too far. Were this so, "going public" would confer an immunity on both nefarious joint undertakings and an absolute protection to criminal enterprise not vouchsafed by the First Amendment even for individual speech.

[22] Military Selective Service Act of 1967, 50-Appendix U.S.C. § 462(a) (Supp. IV, 1969):

> Any person . . . who knowingly counsels, aids, or abets another to refuse or evade registration or service in the armed forces or any of the requirements of this title [said sections], or of said rules, regulations or directions . . . or who conspires to commit any one or more of such offenses, shall, upon conviction in any district court of the United States of competent jurisdiction, be punished by imprisonment for not more than five years or a fine of not more than $10,000, or by both such fine and imprisonment . . . .

[23] 416 F.2d at 168. Spock participated in drawing up A *Call to Resist Illegitimate Authority*, and a cover letter requesting signatures, funds, and a commitment of personal effort to ending the war in Vietnam. Coffin and Spock signed the cover letter and were among the original signers of the *Call*, which later was signed by Goodman and several hundred others. A copy of the *Call* appears in the appendix to the opinion in *Spock*, 416

the surrender and burning of draft cards at Arlington Street Church in Boston,[25] the October 20th antiwar demonstration in Washington,[26] and a march and sit-in at the Whitehall Induction Center in New York.[27]

The opinion expresses a pervasive concern with attempting to make the evil separable from the good in an organization with mixed legal and illegal aims, without inhibiting legitimate organization in an orderly society.[28]

In positing the importance of the first amendment rights of free speech and free association,[29] the court focuses on the nature of the larger grouping from which the four defendants were drawn:

> This intertwining of legal and illegal aspects, the public setting of the agreement and its political purposes, and the loose confederation of possibly innocent and possibly

---

F.2d at 192. It was addressed "To the young men of America, to the whole of the American people, and to men of good will everywhere." It denominated the American war in Vietnam as immoral, unconstitutional, illegal, and violative of international agreements, treaties, and principles of law endorsed by the United States. It also challenged denial of exemption to men whose religious or philosophical beliefs led them to oppose the war as an unconstitutional denial of both religious liberty and equal protection of the laws. On the belief "that every freeman has a legal right and a moral duty to exert every effort to end this war, to avoid collusion with it, and to encourage others to do the same," the signers found the forms of resistance listed (in a form including or suggesting illegal resistance) courageous and justified, and offered their active support.

[24] *Id.* at 177. On October 2, 1967, a press conference was held to publicize the *Call.* Coffin, Goodman and Spock released statements consistent with the *Call.* Goodman advanced his own document, *Civil Disobedience,* which gave as its purpose, "[t]o take away from the government the support and bodies it needs." Coffin was one of the signers of *Civil Disobedience.*

[25] *Id.* at 168, 178. On October 16 a draft card burning and surrender took place at the Arlington Street Church in Boston. It was arranged in part by Ferber. Coffin participated in receiving the draft cards.

[26] *Id.* at 177. On October 20 the four defendants attended an antiwar demonstration in Washington, organized by Goodman and Coffin, where they attempted to turn over their collection of draft cards to the Attorney General. At the Washington demonstration Goodman stated the desire of the older generation to form an alliance with young men which "we will persist in, at least as long as the war lasts, in which we will encourage them and aid and abet and counsel them in every way we know how." At the same demonstration Coffin likewise referred to and approved a joint undertaking: "We hereby publicly counsel these young men to continue in their refusal to serve in the armed forces as long as the war in Vietnam continues, and we pledge ourselves to aid and abet them in all the ways we can." Spock spoke, warning against division in the ranks of the resisters.

[27] On December 5 Spock and Goodman participated in a march and sit-in at the Whitehall Induction Center. Both were arrested. The court did not mention, and apparently did not rely on, the events at the Whitehall Induction Center. The event was cited in the briefs of both sides.

[28] 416 F.2d at 173.

[29] *Id.* at 169, 170.

guilty participants raise the most serious First Amendment problems.[30]

The solution adopted by the court is the addition of a third element, specific individual intent, to the two traditionally required elements of a conspiracy, *i.e.*, agreement and illegal purpose.[31]

In finding an agreement, the court cited the evidence regarding the *Call*, the cover letter, and the press conference—the factual basis of the government's claim of agreement. Concluding that the evidence disclosed more than parallel conduct, the court found the jury justified in inferring an agreement from these instances of concerted activity.[32]

For evidence of illegal purpose the court looked solely to the *Call*, and "its own clues as to what its subscribers may have intended the words to mean."[33] It held that the jury was justified in finding a "call to unlawful refusal,"[34] but was again troubled by the dual purposes of the defendants' actions:

> The Call had a "double aspect: in part it was a denunciation of governmental policy and, in part, it involved a public call to resist the duties imposed by the Act."[35]

Finally, the element added by the court, specific illegal intent of each defendant, is discussed extensively. A standard for judging the requisite intent is set—"strictissimi juris"[36]—to distinguish those guilty of the crime of conspiracy from others in a group with mixed legal and illegal aims. Specific illegal intent of each defendant, the court found, may be manifested by: (1) prior or subsequent unambiguous statements; (2) subsequent commission of the illegal activities contemplated by the agreement; (3) subsequent legal act, if such act is "clearly undertaken for the specific purpose of rendering effective the later illegal activity which is advocated."[37] The factual inquiry was broad, looking beyond the *Call* and press conference, which were the focus in finding the agreement and unlawful purpose, to the complete list of antiwar ac-

---

[30] *Id.* at 169.
[31] The court commented:
> Application of such a standard should forcefully answer the defendant's protests that conviction of any of them would establish criminal responsibility of all of the many hundreds of persons who signed the Call. Even if the Call included illegal objectives, there is a wide gap between signing a document such as the Call and demonstrating one's personal attachment to illegality.

Id. at 173.
[32] *Id.* at 175.
[33] *Id.* at 176.
[34] *Id.*
[35] *Id.*, the court quoting from the Unitarian Universalist Association, amicus on behalf of Ferber.
[36] *Id.* at 172. Defined as: "[o]f the strictist right or law." BLACK'S LAW DICTIONARY 1591 (4th ed. 1951).
[37] *Id.* at 173.

tivities in which the defendants were involved.[38]

Applying the above tests, the court failed to find the requisite specific illegal intent for Spock and Ferber.[39] Coffin and Goodman, however, were remanded for retrial on the prejudicial error of the judge below in submitting specific questions to the jury.[40]

III.   United States v. Spock: The Logic

A court should be compelled by the logic it adopts to reach a result consistent with that logic. If it fails to do so, the opinion may yield a confusing precedent.

The majority in *United States v. Spock* ostensibly adopts the logic of *form c* and recognizes that the involvement of first amendment rights requires special protections.[41] Because of the importance of first amendment rights they specifically approve the application of a less restrictive alternative if there is one by which the substantive evil can be prevented.[42] The logic of *form d;* whereby open discussion yields a positive value to society rather than a danger, was rejected.[43]

The disposition of the individual cases is consistent with the court's logic. Ferber and Spock were acquitted. Although the cases of Goodman and Coffin were remanded for new trials, it does not appear that they will be reprosecuted.[44] Careful analysis of the opinion, however, indicates that the court reached its conclusion by reasoning inconsistent with the logic it claimed:

(1) In indicating the appropriateness of a less restrictive alternative because of first amendment involvement, the court relied on a weighing process. As Judge Coffin indicates in his dissent, however, its attention focused on only one side of the balance.[45] It

---

[38] *Id.* at 176-79. For specific intent, the court looked to the Arlington Street Church ceremony, the Washington demonstration and Goodman's *Civil Disobedience,* as well as the *Call* and the press conference.

[39] *Id.* at 179. Spock's actions supposedly lacked the clear character necessary to imply specific intent. Ferber, although he made incidental use of some of the other defendants' purposes, did not show a commitment to all of them. The court found that while he might be guilty of a smaller conspiracy, he should not be convicted for the larger one.

[40] *Id.* at 180-83. The use of such questions was held to be a simple way to force a verdict of guilty, by making guilt the logical result of the answers given to the questions. The jury, as the conscience of the community, should be permitted to make its decision independent of the logical compulsion of the jury instructions.

[41] *Id.* at 170.

[42] *Id.*

[43] *Id.*

[44] This was the opinion expressed by Leonard B. Boudin, attorney for Dr. Spock, in a letter dated September 29, 1969. Marshall Tamor Golding, attorney for the Department of Justice, gave no clear indication of plans for retrial in this letter of September 26, 1969.

[45] 416 F.2d at 189.

considered the nation's interest in raising an army; the right of the government, because of the potency of conspiratorial conduct, not to have to wait for the commission of the substantive offense; the incitement of defendants' actions; and the fact that Congress has authorized the crime of conspiracy as a sanction. There is no discussion of the efficacy of less restrictive alternatives.[46] Nor were specific aspects of first amendment involvement weighed. The court concludes:

> The First Amendment cases merely present a more difficult problem of insuring that the government does not use its procedural advantages to expand the strict elements of the offense.[47]

(2) After finding that the government's interest in opposing a less restrictive alternative was overwhelming, the court set out a method of protecting first amendment rights when the conspiracy doctrine is applied. However, their reasoning and their language appear to yield a broader liability than is provided for a non-first amendment conspiracy prosecution.

Rather than raising the threshold requirement of a combination, for a conspiracy or at least an agreement, the court summarily accepted the jury's finding of an agreement and turned to the evidence of specific intent to ensure the culpability of the individual members of the alleged conspiracy. The court presumed that an agreement was sufficient to yield a conspiracy,[48] and then accepted the jury's finding of an agreement from instances of allegedly concerted activity.

> The Call was not what is known in law as an integrated document, limited to the four corners of the instrument. The jury could properly infer that it could not occur in the abstract, with no parents, and no active participants in a joint undertaking. We hold that they could look to Spock as one of the drafters, and to Spock and Coffin as two of the four signers of the solicitation letter, and in light of the press conference held to publicize the Call in which Goodman took a prominent part, they could find that Goodman included himself as an active member.[49]

Consequently, the court deprives "agreement" of much of its significance in a case where the agreement or combination among the

---

[46] *Id.* at 190 (Coffin, J., dissenting).
   Nowhere does the court indicate why either approach (individual or collective prosecution for the substantive crime) could not have served the societal interest equally as well. If "less restrictive alternative" is to have any real meaning courts should examine with specificity the utility of the rifle before resort is had to the shotgun.
   Id.
[47] *Id.* at 172.
[48] *See* text accompanying notes 9-10, *supra.*
[49] 416 F.2d at 175.

parties is crucial to the finding of a conspiracy.[50]

Treating the agreement, even when established, as an insufficient predicate[51] is inconsistent with the emphasis in the law of conspiracy upon the relationship among individuals. To look at individual acts for specific intent does not focus on the conspiracy. The Court listed certain facts which might be evidence of specific intent: prior or subsequent unambiguous statements by defendant, subsequent commission by defendant of the illegal act contemplated by the agreement, or subsequent legal acts of defendant clearly undertaken to make the later activity effective.[52] The last two refer to the agreement, but the concentration on specific intent regarding the agreement weakens this essential aspect of conspiracy. The focus of the *Spock* court is on the individual rather than the conspiracy; and the subsequent actions of the defendants, and not the agreement, become crucial. The result is a form of substantive offense prosecution[53] which carries penalties intended for the additional danger caused by the collective action of a conspiracy.

IV. CONCLUSION

The underlying assumption of the doctrine of conspiracy, that increased danger to society results from collective action, requires that two elements form the offense—(a) relationship among individuals sufficient to produce collective action, and (b) an unlawful purpose which adds the dimension of increased danger. The court in *Spock* presumed a sufficient agreement for a conspiracy and granted that first amendment rights call for special protection. However, the court chose to protect the alleged conspirators in circumstances involving first amendment rights by considering the specific individual intent. If this were linked with sufficient evidence of an agreement, then the result might have been consistent. However, the derogation of the element of an agreement places the individual in the position of being tried for a substantive offense rather than the alleged crime of conspiracy. The doctrine that emerges has, arguably, exceeded the limits of its logic, and has increased the threat of conspiracy prosecution as a weapon to control political dissent.[54]

---

[50] *Id.* at 187 (Coffin, J., dissenting).
[51] *Id.* at 190 (Coffin, J., dissenting).
[52] *Id.* at 173.
[53] *Id.* at 190 (Coffin, J., dissenting).
[54] As Judge Coffin expressed in his dissent:
   This is a landmark case and no one, I take it, supposes that this will be the last attempt by the government to use the conspiracy weapon. The government has cast a wide net and caught only two fish. My objection is not that more were not caught but that the government can try again on another day in another court and the court's rationale provides no meaningful basis for predicting who will find themselves within the net. Finally there is the greater danger that the casting of the net has scared away many whom the government had no right to catch.
Id. at 191 (Coffin, J., dissenting).

EVIDENCE—PRIOR INCONSISTENT STATEMENTS OF A WIT-
NESS AS SUBSTANTIVE EVIDENCE—Gelhaar v. State, 41 Wis.
2d 230, 163 N.W.2d 609 (1969). The defendant fatally stabbed her
husband after an extended and bitter argument. The latter part
of the argument, which occurred in the defendant's house, was
heard by her two children, aged 15 and 17, who were upstairs in
their bedrooms. As part of the police investigation, the children
were questioned about what they had heard; the police notes of the
statements tended to show intent to kill. At the trial the children
gave testimony which supported a plea of self-defense. When
questioned about their earlier statements to the officers, the children admitted making statements but denied any recollection of the
content. The police notes from the investigation were then introduced as evidence. The jury instructions did not limit the evidentiary value of these notes to impeachment purposes.[1] The defendant was found guilty of first-degree murder and sentenced to life
imprisonment.

On appeal the defendant argued that the trial court had erred
in not instructing the jury that the prior statements could be used
only to impeach the witnesses' testimony and not as substantive
evidence.[2] In rejecting this argument the Wisconsin Supreme Court
held that, with certain safeguards, prior inconsistent statements by
non-party witnesses may be considered as substantive evidence by
the trier-of-fact. Prior decisions to the contrary were expressly
overruled.[3]

The court considered the hearsay rule as the primary objection
to admitting prior statements as substantive evidence.[4] The theory
of the objection is that the statement is inadmissible as substantive
evidence because the witness was neither under oath nor subject
to cross-examination at the time it was made.[5] The court, never-

---

[1] Evidently the defense attorney did not object when the notes were
introduced nor did he ask the judge to limit their evidentiary value to
impeachment purposes. He also failed to request an instruction on the
value that the jury should accord to these notes, and the court did not give
one *sua sponte*.

[2] The defendant also argued that without the prior statements of her
children, there was no competent evidence to show intent and that the conviction for first degree murder should be overturned.

[3] It appears the court was a little overanxious in its desire to adopt
the new rule. The court admitted in the second half of the opinion that the
conviction was supported by adequate evidence even if the prior statements
were excluded as substantive evidence. Since the *Gelhaar* rule was unnecessary to the decision, it is technically dictum.

[4] 58 AM. JUR. *Witnesses* § 74 (1948); C. McCORMICK, McCORMICK ON
EVIDENCE § 39, at 74 (1954) [hereinafter cited as McCORMICK]; 3 J. WIGMORE,
EVIDENCE § 1018, at 687 (3d ed. 1940) [hereinafter cited as WIGMORE].
Prior inconsistent statements are not hearsay when used to impeach a wit-
ness. See Hamilton v. Reinemann, 233 Wis. 572, 578, 290 N.W. 194, 197
(1940).

[5] McCORMICK 75; WIGMORE 687.

theless, felt that there were several compelling reasons for adopting the new rule, and relied on legal scholars rather than case law as primary support for its position.[6] First, the new rule meets the hearsay objection concerning cross-examination.

> Here, however, by hypothesis the witness is present and subject to cross-examination. There is ample opportunity to test him as to the basis for his former statement. The whole purpose of the Hearsay rule has been already satisfied.[7]

Second, because the prior statement is made nearer in time to the event, it is usually more truthful and accurate than later testimony, and is less subject to various external pressures.[8] Finally, juries seldom are able to make the distinction between impeaching testimony and substantive evidence; generally they use evidence or testimony in any manner that they choose.[9]

The rule and the safeguards adopted by the Wisconsin Supreme Court are basically those proposed by McCormick:

> A statement made on a former occasion by a declarant having an opportunity to observe the facts stated, will be received as evidence of such facts, notwithstanding the rule against hearsay if
> (1) the statement is proved to have been written or signed by the declarant, or to have been given by him as testimony in a judicial or official hearing, or the making of the statement is acknowledged by the declarant in his testimony in the present proceeding, and
> (2) the party against whom the statement is offered is afforded an opportunity to cross-examine the declarant.[10]

The court also added a restriction of its own. It limited the rule to impeachment situations by requiring that: "(3) the witness

---

[6] The court quoted extensively from McCORMICK and WIGMORE, *supra*, note 4.

[7] WIGMORE 687-8, quoted in Gelhaar v. State, 41 Wis. 2d 230, 239, 163 N.W.2d 609, 612 (1969); *see also* McCORMICK 75.

[8] McCORMICK 75-6, quoted in Gelhaar v. State, 41 Wis. 2d 230, 239, 163 N.W.2d 609, 613 (1969).

[9] McCORMICK 77, quoted *id.* at 240, 163 N.W.2d at 613.

[10] McCORMICK 82, quoted *id.* at 241, 163 N.W.2d at 614. The rule at this point is similar to the MODEL CODE OF EVIDENCE rule 503 (1942) which states: "Evidence of a hearsay declaration is admissible if the judge finds that the declarant . . . (b) is present and subject to cross-examination. This position is also taken by the UNIFORM RULES OF EVIDENCE which purports to follow the MODEL CODE OF EVIDENCE. It lists as an exception to the Hearsay rule:

> (1) *Previous Statements of Persons Present and Subject to Cross Examination.* A statement made by a person who is present at the hearing and available for cross examination with respect to the statement and its subject matter, provided the statement would be admissible if made by declarant while testifying as a witness . . . .

UNIFORM RULES OF EVIDENCE rule 63 (1) (1953).

has testified to the same events in a contrary manner in the present proceedings."[11] This restriction also results in excluding prior *consistent* statements from the scope of the new rule.[12] The court reserved judgment concerning hostile witnésses since *impeachment* of one's own witness is still controlled by statute in criminal cases.[18] Thus, the rule at present is limited to adverse party witnesses.

I. DISCUSSION

Prior to *Gelhaar* the law in Wisconsin was well settled: prior inconsistent statements by non-party witnesses were strictly limited to impeachment purposes.[14] However, if the witness was a party to the action and the admission was against his interest, the prior inconsistent statement could be admitted as substantive evidence.[15]

The *Gelhaar* rule has not been adopted by any other court, state or federal, in the country. With a few minor exceptions, every other jurisdiction follows the rule just abandoned in Wisconsin.[16] The exceptions are isolated cases or slight variations in the general rule. For example, Missouri allows depositions to be used as substantive evidence because they are given under oath and the witness is subject to cross-examination at the time of the deposition.[17]

---

[11] 41 Wis. 2d at 241, 163 N.W.2d at 614.

[12] As the court notes, McCORMICK and the MODEL CODE OF EVIDENCE would include prior *consistent* statements within the rule. The UNIFORM RULES OF EVIDENCE would be in agreement. *Supra*, note 9.

[18] WIS. STAT. § 885.35 (1967) states:

> *Hostile witness in criminal cases.* Where testimony of a witness on the trial in a criminal action is inconsistent with a statement previously made by him and reduced to writing and approved by him or taken by a phonographic reporter, he may, in the discretion of the court, be regarded as a hostile witness and examined as an adverse witness, and the party producing him may impeach him by evidence of such prior contradictory statement.

As interpreted in State v. Major, 274 Wis. 110, 79 N.W.2d 75 (1956), this statute prohibits use of a hostile witness' prior inconsistent statement as substantive evidence. Since the court specifically deferred judgment concerning a *hostile* witness in a *civil* case, the probable implication is that the new rule covers *adverse* witnesses in criminal *and* civil cases. Gelhaar v. State, 41 Wis. 2d 230, 242 n.4, 163 N.W.2d 609, 615 n.4 (1969).

[14] Foryan v. Fireman's Fund Ins. Co., 27 Wis. 2d 133, 133 N.W.2d 724 (1965); State v. Major, 274 Wis. 110, 79 N.W.2d 75 (1956); Jaster v. Miller, 269 Wis. 223, 69 N.W.2d 265 (1955); Hamilton v. Reinemann, 233 Wis. 572, 290 N.W. 194 (1940).

[15] Ianni v. Grain Dealers Mut. Ins. Co., 42 Wis. 2d 354, 166 N.W.2d 148 (1969) (post *Gelhaar*); Bach v. Liberty Mut. Fire Ins. Co., 36 Wis. 2d 72, 152 N.W.2d 911 (1967); Steffes v. Farmers Mut. Auto Ins. Co., 7 Wis. 2d 321, 96 N.W.2d 501 (1959); Haney v. Chicago & N.W. Ry., 213 Wis. 670, 252 N.W. 173 (1934); Leslie v. Knudson, 205 Wis. 517, 238 N.W. 397 (1931).

[16] 133 A.L.R. 1454, 1455 (1941); 98 C.J.S. *Witnesses* § 628 (1957); McCORMICK 73; WIGMORE 688.

[17] Ridnour v. Duncan, 291 S.W.2d 900 (Mo. 1956); Snowwhite v. Metropolitan Life Ins. Co., 344 Mo. 705, 127 S.W.2d 718 (1939); Pulitzer v. Chapman, 337 Mo. 298, 85 S.W.2d 400 (1935); Stottlemyre v. Missouri Pac. R.R., 358 S.W.2d 437 (Kansas City Ct. App. 1962).

Some jurisdictions allow prior inconsistent statements to be used as substantive evidence if the truth of the prior statement is admitted at the trial.[18] Others allow use of prior inconsistent statements in an administrative proceeding.[19]

The Wisconsin Supreme Court, however, was not the first court to challenge the validity of the rule limiting prior inconsistent statements by non-party witnesses to impeachment purposes. Judge Friendly, in *United States v. De Sisto*,[20] stated that:

> The rule limiting use of prior statements by a witness subject to cross examination to their effect on his credibility has been described by eminent scholars and judges as "Pious fraud," "artificial," "basically misguided," "mere verbal ritual," and an anachronism "that still impede(s) our pursuit of the truth." [T]o tell a jury it may consider the prior testimony as reflecting on the veracity of the later denial . . . but not as the substantive evidence . . . is a demand for mental gymnastics of which jurors are happily incapable.[21]

Other isolated cases, primarily in the federal courts,[22] have expressed similar dissatisfaction.

II. CONSTITUTIONAL QUESTION

The opinion in *Gelhaar* relied heavily on the support of legal scholars rather than on case law. Thus the Wisconsin Supreme Court apparently considered the hearsay rule as the only objection to the change and concluded that there were sufficient compelling reasons to override this objection. However, a further objection has been considered in two recent California Supreme Court decisions.[23]

---

[18] *E.g.*, Harman v. United States, 199 F.2d 34 (4th Cir. 1952); People v. York, 242 Cal. App. 2d 560, 51 Cal. Rptr. 661 (1966); Schratt v. Fila, 371 Mich. 248, 123 N.W.2d 780 (1963); State v. Davis, 400 S.W.2d 141 (Mo. 1966), *cert. denied*, 385 U.S. 872 (1966).

[19] *E.g.*, Gee Nee Way v. McGrath, 111 F.2d 327 (9th Cir. 1940) (immigration and naturalization proceeding); United States *ex rel.* Ng Kee Wong v. Corsi, 65 F.2d 564 (2d Cir. 1933) (immigration and naturalization proceeding); Rowe v. Goldberg Film Delivery Lines, 50 Ariz. 349, 72 P.2d 432 (1937) (state industrial commission).

[20] 329 F.2d 929 (2d Cir. 1964), *cert. denied*, 377 U.S. 979 (1964).

[21] *Id.* at 933. Judge Friendly affirmed the decision of the district judge who allowed the previous testimony of the witness to be used as substantive evidence. This testimony was given at a previous trial where the witness was under oath and subject to cross-examination.

[22] *E.g.*, Benson v. United States, 402 F.2d 576, 581 n.13 (9th Cir. 1968); Copes v. United States, 345 F.2d 723 (D.C. Cir. 1964); United States v. Allied Stevedoring Corp., 241 F.2d 925 (2d Cir. 1957); United States v. Schwartz, 252 F. Supp. 866 (E.D. Pa. 1966), *rev'd*, 390 F.2d 1 (3d Cir. 1968) (dissatisfaction at district court level); State v. Jolly, 112 Mont. 352, 116 P.2d 686 (1941) (dictum).

[23] People v. Green, 70 Cal. 2d 654, 451 P.2d 422, 75 Cal. Rptr. 782 (1969),

Until recently, California followed "the general common law rule . . . limiting admission of prior inconsistent statements in *criminal cases* to impeachment purposes."[24] In 1965 the California legislature adopted a new comprehensive Evidence Code. Section 1235 of this code provides:

> Evidence of a statement made by a witness is not made inadmissible by the hearsay rule if the statement is inconsistent with his testimony at the hearing and is offered in compliance with Section 770.[25]

The legislative comments to this section suggest an interpretation very similar to the rule adopted in *Gelhaar*.[26]

This section of the statute received a very chilly reception in the California Supreme Court. In *People v. Johnson*[27] and again in *People v. Green*,[28] that court held that § 1235 is unconstitutional as applied to criminal trials.[29] The scope of the constitutional prohibition was explained in *Green*:

> In summary, the rules that emerge from the cases and principles are these: cross-examination at trial relating to a statement or testimony given previously is constitutionally inadequate. (Johnson.)[30] Cross-examination at the time of the statement, e.g., at a preliminary hearing, before a judge or agency other than the trier of fact charged with the ultimate determination of credibility and guilt, is likewise constitutionally inadequate. (Barber.)[31] A combination of these two negatives obviously cannot produce a positive. Therefore, cross-examination at trial on prior testimony, together with cross-examination at the time of the statement before a different trier of fact, is not a valid substitute for constitutionally adequate confrontation.[32]

The practical effect of these cases is to exclude everything but trial testimony as substantive evidence.

---

cert. granted, 396 U.S. 1001 (1970); and People v. Johnson, 68 Cal. 2d 646, 441 P.2d 111, 68 Cal. Rptr. 599 (1968).

[24] People v. Green, 70 Cal. 2d 654, 659, 451 P.2d 422, 425, 75 Cal. Rptr. 782, 785 (1969) (emphasis added).

[25] CAL. EVID. CODE § 1235 (West 1966). (Section 770 states that the witness must be given a chance to explain or deny the previous statement, or he must still be on the stand.)

[26] *Id.*, Comment.

[27] People v. Johnson, 68 Cal. 2d 646, 441 P.2d 111, 68 Cal. Rptr. 599 (1968).

[28] People v. Green, 70 Cal. 2d 654, 451 P.2d 422, 75 Cal. Rptr. 782 (1969).

[29] *People v. Green* and *People v. Johnson* invalidated section 1235 of the California Evidence Code only in criminal cases. There is apparently no constitutional objection to the section as applied to civil cases.

[30] People v. Johnson, 68 Cal. 2d 646, 441 P.2d 111, 68 Cal. Rptr. 599 (1968).

[31] Barber v. Page, 390 U.S. 719 (1968).

[32] People v. Green, 70 Cal. 2d 654, 665, 451 P.2d 422, 429, 75 Cal. Rptr. 782, 789 (1969).

The California Supreme Court claimed that its interpretation of the sixth amendment right to confront witnesses was a logical consequence of three recent United States Supreme Court decisions: *Pointer v. Texas*,[33] *Barber v. Page*,[34] and *Berger v. California*.[35] In each case, the witness did not appear at the trial, and his previous statements were admitted as substantive evidence.[36] The United States Supreme Court reversed all three convictions on the same ground—the prosecution did not make a reasonable attempt to secure the attendance of the witness at the trial.[37] It held that the right to cross-examine witnesses required cross-examination before the trier-of-fact, *if possible*, so the jury could observe the witness' demeanor and hear his explanation of the inconsistency between his prior statement and his trial testimony. However, these cases did not require cross-examination contemporaneous with the making of the statement if the witness was present at the trial.

Apparently the California Supreme Court concluded that the language of the three federal cases implied much more than their immediate holdings.[38] In reaching this conclusion, it either ignored or overlooked another recent United States Supreme Court decision, *Douglas v. Alabama*.[39] In this case, the witness denied making the prior statement and refused to answer any questions about it. The Court reversed the conviction, stating: "Hence, effective confrontation of Loyd was possible only if Loyd affirmed the statement as his."[40] Thus the Court implies that it is possible to have constitutionally adequate confrontation if the witness admits making the statement. This implication is in direct conflict with the conclusion of the California Supreme Court that the cross-examination *must* take place *when* the statement is made.

However, the United States Supreme Court had, less than two decades earlier, rendered a decision similar in effect to the Cali-

[33] 380 U.S. 400 (1965).
[34] 390 U.S. 719 (1968).
[35] 393 U.S. 314 (1969).
[36] In *Barber v. Page* and *Berger v. California* the witness was cross-examined at the preliminary hearing. No counsel was present at the preliminary hearing in *Pointer v. Texas*, although the defendant attempted to cross-examine the witness.
[37] In *Pointer v. Texas* and *Berger v. California* the witness lived out of state while in *Barber v. Page* the witness was serving a sentence in a federal prison. The decision in *Pointer v. Texas* also held that the sixth amendment right to confrontation was applicable to the states by operation of the fourteenth amendment. Wisconsin has required *diligent* efforts on the part of the prosecution to secure the attendance of witnesses at criminal trials. Inda v. State, 198 Wis. 557, 224 N.W. 733 (1929).
[38] For an attack on the reasoning of the California Supreme Court in *People v. Johnson*, see Note, 15 WAYNE L. REV. 874 (1969).
[39] 380 U.S. 415 (1965).
[40] *Id.* at 420.

fornia decisions. In *Bridges v. Wixon*[41] it said:

> We may assume they [prior inconsistent statements] would be admissible for purposes of impeachment. But they certainly would not be admissible in any criminal case as substantive evidence. So to hold would allow men to be convicted on unsworn testimony of witnesses—a practice which runs counter to the notions of fairness on which our legal system is founded.[42]

While *Douglas v. Alabama* possibly overrules *Bridges v. Wixon*, the implication in the former case may be the result of imprecise language rather than any desire to overrule *Bridges*.[43]

The Wisconsin Supreme Court did not deal with the Sixth Amendment problem considered in *Pointer v. Texas*, *Barber v. Page*, and *People v. Johnson* although these cases were decided before *Gelhaar*. This problem has, however, been considered by the Committee on Rules of Practice and Procedure of the Judicial Conference of the United States. In its *Preliminary Draft of Proposed Rules of Evidence for the United States District Courts and Magistrates*,[44] the committee reviewed the available cases and commentaries, and proposed a broader rule than that established by the Wisconsin court.[45] The advisory committee discussed *People v. Johnson* and specifically rejected it in favor of McCormick's reasoning and the comments to section 1235 of the *California Evidence Code*.[46] Although the *Proposed Rules* have not yet been adopted by the United States Supreme Court, the committee's recommendation lends considerable support to the Wisconsin position.

---

[41] 326 U.S. 135 (1945).

[42] *Id.* at 153-54. *Accord* Goings v. United States, 377 F.2d 753 (8th Cir. 1967) which states: "The right to confront the witness at the time the statements are made is paramount in a criminal trial." 377 F.2d at 762 n.12.

[43] It might even be possible to reconcile the two cases. *See* the *Preliminary Draft of Proposed Rules of Evidence for the United States District Courts and Magistrates*, 46 F.R.D. 161, 328 (1969) where it is suggested that *Bridges v. Wixon* could be read narrowly as merely reversing the Immigration and Naturalization Service for not following its own rules. Such an interpretation would not conflict with *Douglas v. Alabama*.

[44] 46 F.R.D. 161 (1969).

[45] *Preliminary Draft of Proposed Rules of Evidence for the United States District Courts and Magistrates* rule 8.01(c)(1)-(2) (1969) states:

> (c) HEARSAY. "Hearsay" is a statement, offered in evidence to prove the truth of the matter asserted, unless
>   (1) TESTIMONY AT HEARING. The statement is one made by a witness while testifying at the trial or hearing; or
>   (2) PRIOR STATEMENT BY WITNESS. The declarant testifies at the trial or hearing and is subject to cross-examination concerning the statement, and the statement is (i) inconsistent with his testimony, or (ii) consistent with his testimony and is offered to rebut an express or implied charge against him of recent fabrication or improper influence or motive, or (iii) one of identification of a person made soon after perceiving him, or (iv) a transcript of testimony given under oath at a trial or hearing or before a grand jury . . . .

[46] 46 F.R.D. at 337.

III. CONCLUSION

The California opinions raise constitutional questions which should be considered by the Wisconsin Supreme Court in criminal cases.[47] However, there are compelling policy arguments to support the rule adopted in *Gelhaar*: the prior statement is closer to the actual event and therefore probably more accurate; there is less chance for subtle or overt pressures on the witness between the incident and statement; and the jury will seldom differentiate between impeachment and substantive evidence.

The impact of the *Gelhaar* rule on other jurisdictions is uncertain at present. Technically it is only dictum even in Wisconsin. But the manner in which the Wisconsin Supreme Court proposed the new rule, including the express overruling of all earlier cases to the contrary, leaves little doubt that the court will continue to follow it.

CONSTITUTIONAL LAW—PRETRIAL PUBLICITY—THE MILWAUKEE 14—United States v. Cotton, No. 68-CR-113 (E.D. Wis. June 11, 1969). In September 1968, defendants, a group that would later be known as the Milwaukee 14, entered a Milwaukee selective service office, removed registrants' records, and burned them as a protest against the Vietnam war. In conjunction with the destruction of these records, they issued a press release declaring the purpose of their actions.[1] Widespread publicity accompanied their convictions eight months later on state charges of burglary, theft, and arson.[2] Subseqently, they faced federal prosecution for destroying

[47] In addition to the problems presented by the California cases, the ruled adopted in *Gelhaar* faces one other possible challenge. Under the new rule, a prior inconsistent statement can be admitted as substantive evidence if the jury decides that the statement was made or signed by the witness. In such a case, if the witness were to still deny making the statement, use of it as substantive evidence would violate the defendant's right to confrontation since he would have been precluded from cross-examining the witness at the trial. *See* Douglas v. Alabama, 380 U.S. 415 (1965); *accord* Bruton v. United States, 391 U.S. 123 (1968).

[1] The following statement was given to newsmen:
We who burn these records of our society's war machine are participants in a movement of resistance to slavery, a struggle that remains as unresolved in America as in most of the world.
Our act concentrates on the selective service system because its relation to murder is immediate. Men are drafted—or "volunteer" for fear of being drafted—as killers for the state. Their victims litter the planet.
Today we destroy selective service system files because men need to be reminded that property is not sacred . . . . If anything tangible is sacred, it is the gift of life and flesh.
Milwaukee Journal, Sept. 25, 1968, § 1, at 1, col. 2.
[2] Milwaukee Journal, May 27, 1969, § 1, at 1, col. 5. Defendants were subsequently sentenced to two years in the Wisconsin State Prison. Milwaukee Journal, June 7, 1969, § 1, at 1, col. 4.

government records, interfering with the operation of the selective service system, and conspiring to commit these offenses. The widespread, and frequently hostile, publicity continued in all news media to the time of the federal trial. During this time, the defendants themselves encouraged publicity and issued additional press releases.[3]

At the commencement of the federal proceedings only ten defendants remained. Three had pleaded guilty[4] and another was to be tried separately.[5] A fifteenth defendant, Hagedorn, had petitioned for and had been granted a change of venue on the ground of community prejudice.[6] Materials relating alleged hostile coverage by the press, radio, and television were submitted with this petition. The remaining defendants subsequently moved for dismissal because of community prejudice. The court denied the motion and indicated that it required a judicial evaluation other than that used for change of venue. It noted that a motion to dismiss could not be granted prior to the voir dire examination of prospective jurors.[7] Defendants were invited by the court to seek a change of venue, but they declined to do so.

In attempting to select an impartial jury, the court screened 142 potential jurors, 137 of them individually.[8] Virtually all of them were familiar with the Milwaukee 14 and, by their own admissions, had been exposed to hostile discussions concerning the defendants. Furthermore, most were aware of the previous state convictions. Although some prospective jurors expressed a lack of prejudice, the court determined that they were in fact biased. Concluding that an impartial jury could not be selected at that time, the court held that the defendants could not receive a fair trial and granted the motion to dismiss.[9]

---

[3] The defendants' intention was to create a forum for discussion of the Vietnam conflict; therefore, publicity was necessary to achieve their goal. In fact, one defendant later pleaded guilty in federal court because he did not think that the state trial had proved to be a successful forum for debate on the morality of the war. Milwaukee Journal, June 10, 1969, § 1, at 1, col. 5.

[4] The first defendant to plead guilty was sentenced to one year imprisonment for interference with the selective service system; the other charges were dropped. Milwaukee Journal, June 4, 1969, § 1, at 1, col. 4.

[5] Milwaukee Journal, June 5, 1969, § 1, at 19, col. 6.

[6] Hagedorn was not directly involved in the destruction of the draft records and thus not one of the "14." He was the intermediary who led newsmen to the scene of the burning. Milwaukee Journal, Sept. 26, 1968, § 1, at 1, col. 4.

[7] United States v. Cotton, No. 68-CR-113 (E.D. Wis., June 11, 1969). The judge issued an oral memorandum opinion which is included in the trial transcript.

[8] The court had questioned the first five prospective jurors as a group. The remaining 137 were interrogated separately and in the absence of other jurors. Id.

[9] Id. A petition seeking a writ of mandamus ordering the district

In dismissing the charges the court indicated there were three ways to guarantee a fair trial in the face of prejudice created by widespread, hostile publicity in the community: change of venue, continuance, or elimination of the prejudiced jurors through voir dire examination. The court found that change of venue and continuance clashed with the defendants' right to a speedy trial in the district where the alleged offenses were committed.[10] Because these rights have a constitutional basis, the court felt that they could be waived only by motion of the defendants. Since the defendants had declined to do so, and since voir dire had failed to produce an impartial jury, the court considered dismissal to be the only appropriate remedy.[11]

In concluding that the community prejudice in Milwaukee prevented a fair trial in the district at that time, the court did not consider the source of publicity relevant. Whatever the source, the effect on potential jurors was the significant factor. Thus any contribution to the publicity by the defendants was irrelevant to the motion to dismiss.

It may be argued that *Cotton* permits an accused to force a dismissal in a case attended by hostile publicity by asserting his rights to a proper venue and a speedy trial. The generally accepted principle has been that dismissal is not an appropriate remedy for overcoming pretrial community prejudice.[12] This is based on the constitutional interpretation that proper venue and speedy trial are not absolute rights; rather, they are procedural rights which may be waived[13] to assure the primary right to a fair trial.[14] In fact, it has been suggested that a court may *sua sponte* change venue or continue the case to insure the paramount right to a fair trial.[15]

---

court to reinstate the indictment was denied in United States v. Gordon, No. 17997 (7th Cir., Nov. 26, 1969). The court said mandamus was an inappropriate remedy since a direct appeal to the United States Supreme Court would lie under 18 U.S.C. § 3731 (1964) and the Supreme Court denied review, United States v. Gordon, 38 U.S.L.W. 3314 (U.S. Feb. 24, 1970). The direct appeal was dismissed in United States v. Cotton, 90 S. Ct. 816 (1970).

[10] U.S. CONST. amend. VI.
[11] United States v. Cotton, No. 68-CR-113 (E.D. Wis., June 11, 1969).
[12] Courts generally consider change of venue, continuance, new trial, or reversal the only remedies for pretrial community prejudice. *See* Sheppard v. Maxwell, 384 U.S. 333 (1966); United States v. Zovluck, 274 F. Supp. 385, 389 (S.D.N.Y. 1967); Commonwealth v. Geagan, 339 Mass. 457, 159 N.E.2d 870 (1959), *cert. denied*, 361 U.S. 895 (1959); 16 DePaul L. Rev. 203 (1965).
[13] Hilderbrandt v. United States, 304 F.2d 716 (10th Cir. 1962); Thomas v. United States, 267 F.2d 1 (5th Cir. 1959); Earnest v. United States, 198 F.2d 561 (6th Cir. 1952); Comment, *The Impartial Jury—Twentieth Century Dilemma: Some Solutions to the Conflict between Free Press and Fair Trial*, 51 CORNELL L. REV. 306, 314 (1966).
[14] United States v. Hinton, 268 F. Supp. 728, 731 (E.D. La. 1967); Note, *The Lagging Right to a Speedy Trial*, 51 VA. L. REV. 1587 (1965).
[15] Sheppard v. Maxwell, 384 U.S. 333 (1966). However, the federal

When courts have directly confronted the question of conflict among sixth amendment rights, they have indicated that the accused will be required to waive one of these rights to guarantee that he be brought to trial.[16] In these opinions, dismissal is considered to be such an extreme remedy that it cannot be invoked without a showing that all other remedies would be ineffective.[17] One commonly expressed fear is that dismissal as a remedy would impair the power of law enforcement agencies to repress crime.[18] Another contention is that the primary intent of the sixth amendment is to guarantee a fair trial for the accused, not to provide him with an inalienable right to a trial in his own backyard.[19] The assumption, therefore, is that the necessity of bringing an accused to trial far outweighs any procedural rights he might possess.[20]

Despite the tendency to limit the significance of the rights of venue and a speedy trial, many cases warn against underemphasizing their constitutional importance.[21] These rights are most often described rather generally as substantial rights the accused should not be forced to forego.[22] Some courts consider that a serious constitutional question is presented when a defendant must forego sixth amendment rights to insure a fair trial.[23] Therefore, it cannot, be summarily concluded that dismissal is an improper remedy for prejudicial publicity.

The court's conclusion in *Cotton*—that the voir dire examination had indicated that a fair trial was not possible at that time—rests

---

rules are not conducive to such action by the court. *See* FED. R. CRIM. P. 21. *See also* United States *ex rel.* Darcy v. Handy, 351 U.S. 454 (1956).

[16] Frank v. Mangum, 237 U.S. 309, 337 (1915); State *ex rel.* Schulter v. Roraff, 39 Wis. 2d 342, 159 N.W.2d 25 (1968), *cert. denied*, 393 U.S. 1066 (1969); State v. Woodington, 31 Wis. 2d 151, 142 N.W.2d 810 (1966), *appeal dismissed* and *cert. denied*, 386 U.S. 9 (1967).

[17] State *ex rel.* Schulter v. Roraff, 39 Wis. 2d 342, 159 N.W.2d 25 (1968), *cert. denied*, 393 U.S. 1066 (1969).

[18] Frank v. Mangum, 237 U.S. 309, 337 (1915); State v. Woodington, 31 Wis. 2d 151, 142 N.W.2d 810 (1966), *appeal dismissed* and *cert. denied*, 386 U.S. 9 (1967).

[19] United States v. Hinton, 268 F. Supp. 728 (E.D. La. 1967).

[20] The necessity of bringing an accused to trial makes dismissal a doubtful remedy. Most courts can be expected to circumvent any strong constitutional arguments for dismissal as long as they have other available remedies for juror prejudice. *See* Sheppard v. Maxwell, 384 U.S. 333 (1966).

[21] Klopfer v. North Carolina, 386 U.S. 213, 223 (1967); Salinger v. Loisel, 265 U.S. 224, 232 (1929); Holdridge v. United States, 282 F.2d 302, 305 (8th Cir. 1960); Sullivan, *Prejudicial Publicity: A Look at the Remedies*, 1 SUFFOLK U.L. REV. 77 (1967). There is also a societal interest in a speedy trial. Public anxiety is not fully allayed until a defendant is convicted or acquitted. *See* 45 N. CAR. L. REV. 183 (1966).

[22] *See, e.g.*, Delaney v. United States, 199 F.2d 107, 116 (1st Cir. 1952).

[23] Comment, *Prejudicial Publicity Versus the Rights of the Accused*, 26 LA. L. REV. 818 (1966). *See also* Comment, *supra* note 13.

on firm ground. First, recent Supreme Court decisions have recognized that a prospective juror's prejudice may be assumed under certain circumstances. In *Marhsall v. United States*[24] exposure to portentious, but inadmissible, evidence was considered grounds for dismissing a prospective juror for prejudice. Under the *Marshall* rule, no further inquiry is necessary to determine whether the juror can set aside the impression of such exposure once he admits knowledge of it.[25] In *Cotton*, the prior convictions may well have constituted such portentious, albeit inadmissible, evidence. As a result, a substantial majority of the potential jurors had been exposed and were properly disqualified. Second, extensive publicity from previous litigation could make a subsequent fair trial for the same acts impossible because of a continuing pattern of deep community prejudice.[26] *Cotton*, perhaps, speaks more forcefully for this proposition, since the federal trial immediately followed the state proceedings. The prejudice could not have dissipated significantly in that short interim. Third, the court proceeded to voir dire examination before deciding that community prejudice prevented a fair trial. Consequently, it was consistent with the line of cases indicating that such a determination cannot be made prior to voir dire.[27] Last, it was entirely within the court's discretion to dismiss the case for apparent prejudice. The juror's subjective opinion of his prejudice is not conclusive;[28] ultimately it is the responsibility of the court to decide whether he is prejudiced. This wide discretion[29] made the disposition appropriate in light of deep community prejudice.

---

[24] 360 U.S 310 (1959). Regarding dismissal of prospective jurors and inherent prejudice see Estes v. Texas, 381 U.S. 532 (1965); Turner v. Louisiana, 379 U.S. 466 (1965); Rideau v. Louisiana, 373 U.S. 723 (1963).

[25] The general test for juror prejudice is whether the prospective juror can set aside preconceived notions and try the case solely on the evidence adduced in the trial. Irvin v. Dowd, 366 U.S. 717 (1961). *See also* Patriarca v. United States, 402 F.2d 314 (1st Cir. 1968). The *Marshall* rule would eliminate the prospective juror without a subjective determination of his prejudice. 360 U.S. 310 (1959).

[26] *See* United States *ex rel.* Brown, 200 F. Supp. 885 (D. Ver. 1962), rev'd, 306 F.2d 596 (2d Cir. 1962) (retrial after reversal of conviction); People v. Jenkins, 10 Mich. App. 257, 159 N.W.2d 225 (1968).

[27] Jones v. Gasch, 404 F.2d 1231 (D.C. Cir. 1967), *cert. denied*, 390 U.S. 1029 (1968); Blumenfield v. United States, 284 F.2d 46 (8th Cir. 1960); United States v. Hoffa, 156 F. Supp. 495 (D.D.C. 1957); Shapard v. State, 437 P.2d 565, 578 (Okla. 1967), *cert. denied*, 393 U.S. 826 (1968).

[28] Irvin v. Dowd, 366 U.S. 717, 722 (1960); Silverthorne v. United States, 400 F.2d 627 (9th Cir. 1968); United States v. Largo, 346 F.2d 253 (7th Cir. 1965), *cert. denied*, 382 U.S. 904 (1965).

[29] A court's determination of impartiality can be reversed only on a clear showing of abuse of discretion. Bostick v. United States, 400 F.2d 449 (5th Cir. 1968), *cert. denied*, 393 U.S. 1068 (1969); United States v. Moran, 236 F.2d 361 (2d Cir. 1956), *cert. denied*, 352 U.S. 909 (1956). Thus, while more than 142 jurors have been screened in other cases, it was within the court's discretion to stop at 142.

The court was also on firm ground in determining that the source of publicity was not relevant to the consideration of the defendants' motion. Admittedly, courts may commonly deal unsympathetically with defendants who contribute to the potential denial of their own constitutional rights. This judicial attitude has been reflected in the denial of motions for dismissal because of delay in prosecution where the defendant has been the primary cause of delay.[30] However, in *Cotton* the very purpose of the defendants' actions was to publicize their feelings about the war.[31] They wanted the trial to be a forum for the expression of their views, and pretrial publicity was essential to this goal. It cannot be presumed, therefore, that the intention of the publicity was to make a fair trial impossible. That was caused by hostile publicity emanating from the community.

Additional factors also support the decision in *Cotton*. First, the defendants had already been given two year sentences for the state convictions. Therefore, dismissal did not have the effect of allowing them to escape punishment for their conduct. This is not to suggest that a federal conviction would have subjected the defendants to double jeopardy.[32] However, a prior conviction for the same acts is a significant factor in the second jurisdiction's determination of how to deal equitably with the accused. In fact, there is a trend toward barring a second prosecution for similar offenses.[33]

Second, any delay in prosecution would deprive the defendants of the opportunity to serve the federal and state sentences concurrently.[34] Although the defendants had no legal right to concurrent sentences,[35] the federal government has the authority to allow

---

[30] *See, e.g.,* United States v. Graham, 289 F.2d 352 (7th Cir. 1961); United States v. Lustman, 258 F.2d 475 (2d Cir. 1958), *cert. denied,* 358 U.S. 880 (1958); Fouts v. United States, 253 F.2d 215 (6th Cir. 1958), *cert. denied,* 358 U.S. 884 (1958).

[31] *Supra* note 1.

[32] There is clearly a legal right to prosecute in federal court for acts arising out of the same facts upon which the state prosecution was based. United States v. Lanza, 260 U.S. 377 (1922).

[33] As noted in Bartkus v. Illinois, 359 U.S. 121, 138 n.27 (1959), fifteen states currently have statutes precluding both a state and federal trial for essentially the same offense. Also, there is a greater tendency on the part of prosecutors to decide against prosecution in such situations. Furthermore, Congress has barred prosecution for certain federal offenses after state prosecution for the same acts. *See, e.g.,* 18 U.S.C. § 2117 (1964).

[34] Defendants had been sentenced in state court and were to begin immediately serving the sentence. Milwaukee Journal, June 7, 1969, § 1, at 1, col. 4. The prison term could be delayed only for the federal trial. If there were a postponement, defendants would be returned to state authorities to serve the sentence. Werntz v. Looney, 208 F.2d 102 (10th Cir. 1953).

[35] Hamilton v. Salter, 361 F.2d 579 (4th Cir. 1966); Williams v. Taylor, 327 F.2d 322 (10th Cir. 1964); United States v. Baker, 164 F. Supp. 435 (E.D. Wis. 1958). *See also* Bartkus v. Illinois, 359 U.S. 121 (1959).

a subsequent federal sentence to be served concurrently with a state sentence. The term may even be served in a state prison if the state refuses to relinquish custody until its sentence is served.[36] Because the practice is to frequently allow concurrent sentences,[37] delay would have created a serious, if not expressly recognized, loss.[38] As a result, the right to a speedy trial takes on greater significance since the defendants would have been seriously prejudiced if they had waived it.

Third, the defendants were not criminally assaultive.[39] If the defendants were not imprisoned, any resort to extreme means of expression, which might have resulted from their political philosophy, would have been to property, not to human lives. Consequently, there was a less compelling social interest in keeping these defendants incarcerated. In conclusion, the court's recognition of the substantial rights of proper venue and speedy trial was appropriate for these particular defendants.

The significance of the *Cotton* decision should not be exaggerated, however. The court relied on little case law to support its conclusion. It cited *Sheppard v. Maxwell*[40] in indicating that strong judicial protections must be considered to assure the accused of his constitutional right to a fair trial. It is not at all clear, however, that the Supreme Court in *Sheppard* was suggesting that dismissal was among these measures.[41] Instead, the Court referred to change of venue and continuance as the most extreme remedies to be sought to ensure a fair trial. Nor did the court in *Cotton* cite any case law to support its conclusion that the defendants were not obligated to waive any constitutional rights to obtain a fair trial. It seems unlikely that the court intended to take a definitive stand on the significance of certain procedural rights. It is clear only that the court sought to exercise its discretion in a manner that would achieve justice in this particular case.

Cotton does, however, raise the problem of resolving conflicts

---

[36] Lipscomb v. Stevens, 349 F.2d 997 (6th Cir. 1965), *cert. denied*, 382 U.S. 993 (1966); Williams v. United States, 168 F.2d 866 (5th Cir. 1948); 18 U.S.C. § 4082 (1964).

[37] It is apparent that the defendants in *Cotton* would have received a concurrent federal sentence. Both the courts and the prosecution recognized that a continuance would prejudice them in that respect. United States v. Cotton, No. 68-CR-113 (E.D. Wis., June 11, 1969).

[38] Smith v. Hooey, 393 U.S. 374 (1969); Schindler, *Interjurisdictional Conflict and the Right to a Speedy Trial*, 35 U. Cin. L. Rev. 179, 182 (1966).

[39] The original fourteen consisted of five Roman Catholic priests, one minister in the Founding Church of Scientology, four students, one professor, two draft counselors, and one director of a center for the poor. Milwaukee Journal, *supra* note 1.

[40] 384 U.S 333 (1966).

[41] The Court referred only to the remedies of change of venue, continuance, and new trial. Its reference to "strong measures" come in the context of a discussion of those precautions to be taken in the course of the trial to insure its fairness. *Id.*

among sixth amendment rights. Courts generally have rejected dismissal as a remedy for juror prejudice, but they have been hesitant to go beyond the threshold issue of remedy for such prejudice and deal with the ultimate constitutional question of this conflict of rights. It has been suggested by one author that the rights of proper venue and speedy trial could always be guaranteed if one characterizes an impartial jury as a legal fiction.[42] Under this approach, if the accused fails to move for change of venue or a continuance, the court can proceed to trial with as fair a jury as possible. The obvious danger is that reversal of conviction would be the frequent result if the appellate court's standards of fairness differ from those of the trial court.[43] Consequently, the legal fiction theory provides no answer to the conflicts among sixth amendment rights. A case by case judicial determination of the relationship of these rights is a more compelling approach.

In conclusion, *Cotton* represents a situation where the rights of proper venue and a speedy trial are so valuable to the accused that the extreme remedy of dismissal had to be invoked. But the case does not suggest that there must be a dismissal every time there is a crime of great notoriety. The special considerations involved preclude such a broad reading. Nor does the case mean that venue and a speedy trial are absolute rights; although it does indicate that they are substantial enough to be protected where waiver would unduly burden and prejudice the accused. At a time when freedom of the press and the right to a fair trial are generally preserved at the expense of sixth amendment procedural rights, such a result is encouraging. It considers the significance of constitutional rights whose values have been ignored. While *Cotton* may not establish a trend, it could influence other courts to confront the true nature and relationship of these sixth amendment rights.

CONSUMER PROTECTION—TRUTH IN LENDING AND THE COGNOVIT JUDGMENT—The Truth in Lending Act became effective July 1, 1969.[1] Regulation Z,[2] issued by the Board of Gov-

---

[42] McCarthy, *Fair Trial and Prejudicial Publicity: A Need For Reform*, 17 HASTINGS L.J. 79, 83 (1965). It is argued that disqualification of those actually prejudiced would make it nearly impossible to impanel a jury.

[43] Reversal may be little more than a moral victory for the accused who has been convicted as a result of unfair publicity. Between the trial and the decision on appeal, he has often been deprived of his liberty and has been put to a tremendous ordeal and expense. Segal, *Fair Trial and Free Press—An Analysis of the Problem*, 51 MASS. L.Q. 101 (1966). *See also* Comment, 26 LA. L. REV. 818, *supra* note 23.

---

[1] Consumer Credit Protection Act, 15 U.S.C. §§ 1601-65 (Supp. IV, 1968).

[2] 12 C.F.R. § 226, 34 Fed. Reg. 2002-11 (1969) [hereinafter cited as Reg. Z].

ernors of the Federal Reserve System,[3] put the Act's skeletal provisions into operational form. In accordance with the legislative intent behind the Act, Regulation Z is primarily a disclosure act.[4] It requires creditors[5] to reveal the cost of credit in terms which have a uniformly defined meaning. Both the advertising of credit[6] and the credit transaction itself[7] are governed by disclosure requirements. The legislative intent behind the Truth in Lending Act was a belief that consumers ought to be able to shop for credit as they shop for other goods and services.[8] Presumably, it was thought that a uniform disclosure of interest rates and finance charges would help them do so.

As well as requiring disclosure of credit terms, the Truth in Lending Act creates a new right of rescission.[9] If a creditor retains a security interest in his customer's principal dwelling, the customer has three days in which to rescind the whole transaction.[10] The legislative intention here is more difficult to determine than that behind the disclosure provisions. This unilateral right of rescission is contrary to traditional contract theory. Moreover, it seems inconsistent with commercial conceptions of when a deal is closed. The rescission right can be perceived partly as an attack directed against the "fly-by-night" or "hardsell-quick exit" artist and partly as an expression of a feeling that consumers ought to have a three day cooling off period in any credit transaction secured by their principal dwelling.

The Federal Reserve Board of Governors has interpreted the rescission right and certain disclosure rights of Regulation Z as applicable to those credit transactions in which the debtor authorizes confession of judgment by warrant of attorney.[11] This note will

---

[3] Regulation Z was issued pursuant to the Consumer Credit Protection Act, 15 U.S.C. § 1604 (Supp. IV, 1968).

[4] "It [the Truth in Lending Act] provides for full disclosure of credit charges, rather than regulation of the terms and conditions under which credit may be extended." H.R. REP. No. 1040, 90th Cong., 2d Sess. (1968).

[5] " 'Creditor' means a person who in the ordinary course of business regularly extends or arranges for the extension of consumer credit, or offers to extend or arrange for the extension of such credit." Reg. Z § 226.2(m).

It should also be noted that Regulation Z applies only to those transactions in which credit is extended to natural persons. Commercial credit transactions are not affected by Regulation Z. See Reg. Z § 226.2 (k).

[6] See Reg. Z § 226.10.

[7] See Reg. Z §§ 226.6, 226.7, 226.8.

[8] H.R. REP. No. 1040, 90th Cong., 2d Sess. (1968).

[9] Reg. Z § 226.9.

[10] For exceptions to the rule, see Reg. Z § 226.9(g). The most significant is that there is no right of rescission where the transaction is a purchase money first mortgage on a principal dwelling.

[11] See Truth in Lending Act interpretation letter from J. L. Robert-

discuss the effects of the Truth in Lending Act on Wisconsin cognovit judgment practices and the desirability of those effects in light of the intentions behind the Act.

I. WISCONSIN COGNOVIT JUDGMENTS

A. The Cognovit Statute

In Wisconsin, judgment may be entered against the debtor on a bond or promissory note without commencement of a civil action. *Wisconsin Statutes* section 270.69 provides that a bond or note debtor may authorize any attorney of record to confess judgment for him.[12] Once a creditor has this authorization, he may obtain an enforceable judgment by following the simple procedure outlined in the statute.[13]

The distinctive feature of cognovit procedure is the absence of a requirement for service of process on the defendant debtor. This is possible because the cognovit judgment is the result of a special proceeding rather than a civil action.[14] A debtor will not typically know of the cognovit proceeding until after judgment has been entered against him,[15] but this judgment is enforceable in the same manner as if it were the result of a civil action.[16]

Clearly, the cognovit judgment is a desirable route for bond and note creditors to follow. Indebtedness may be reduced to a

---

son, March 14, 1969, reprinted in 1 CCH CONSUMER CREDIT GUIDE ¶ 3686; *see also* Federal Reserve Press Release (May 26, 1969).

[12]   (1) A judgment upon a bond or promissory note may be rendered, without action, either for money due or to become due, or to secure any person against contingent liability on behalf of the defendant or both, in the manner prescribed in this section.
    (2) The plaintiff shall file his complaint and an answer signed by the defendant or some attorney in his behalf, confessing the amount claimed in the complaint or some part thereof, and such bond or note and, in case such answer is signed by an attorney, an instrument authorizing judgment to be confessed. The plaintiff or some one in his behalf shall make and annex to the complaint an affidavit stating the amount due or to become due on the note or bond, or if such note or bond is given to secure any contingent liability the affidavit must state concisely the facts constituting such liability and must show that the sum confessed does not exceed the same. The judgment shall be signed by the court or a judge and shall be thereupon entered and docketed by the clerk and enforced in the same manner as judgments in other cases.
    (3) Within 30 days after a judgment is entered under sub. (2) the plaintiff shall, by certified mail, transmit notice of entry thereof to the judgment debtor at his last known address. Failure to transmit such notice shall invalidate the judgment.
WIS. STAT. § 270.69 (1967).
[13] WIS. STAT. § 270.69(2) (1967). Forms are available which have the complaint, answer, and affidavit on one document and, therefore, simplify his task even more.
[14] WIS. STAT. § 260.03 (1967).
[15] WIS. STAT. § 270.69(3) (1967).
[16] WIS. STAT. § 270.69(2) (1967).

judgment without the time and expense required in a civil action. Therefore, smart bond and note creditors have always insisted on authorization to confess judgment by a warrant of attorney in the form of a clause written into the instrument which evidences the debt.

But the statute authorizing the Wisconsin cognovit[17] proceeding has been strictly construed.[18] The idea of confession of judgment by warrant of attorney without prior notice to the debtor is contrary to traditional American judicial values,[19] and about the only discernible rationale for the statute is the expediency of the procedure.

Attempts to balance the no notice, no day in court objections against the efficiency of the proceeding are apparent in a number of opinions of the Wisconsin Supreme Court.

B. Note or Bond Requirement

By statute, the cognovit proceeding is available only against bond or note debtors.[20] This limitation mitigates the objections to the denial of a prior judicial hearing. Where the debtor's promise to pay is absolutely unconditional, there is little, if any, possibility of a legal defense to the debt, and the denial of a judicial hearing becomes insignificant. On the other hand, where the promise to pay is conditional, for example in connection with a sales contract, the likelihood of a legal defense increases, and therefore, so does the importance of a judicial hearing.

The problem of deciding when a note, within the meaning of the statute, is severable from a sales contract was considered by the Wisconsin Supreme Court in *United Finance Corp. v. Peterson.*[21] The court construed the word "note" narrowly:

By the word "note" in the statute is meant not a writing

---

[17] The word cognovit undoubtedly derives from the common law procedure of judgment by *cognovit actionem.* After commencement of action the defendant would enter a plea acknowledging and confessing that plaintiff's cause of action was just and rightful. However, confession of judgment by warrant of attorney has always depended on statute for validity and, unlike *cognovit actionem,* it can be used without the prerequisite of commencing civil action. For a history of the cognovit judgment, see 1 H. BLACK, A TREATISE ON THE LAW OF JUDGMENTS 69–73 (2d ed. 1902). *See also* Kahn v. Lesser, 97 Wis. 217, 72 N.W. 739 (1897).

[18] Park Hotel Co. v. Eckstein-Miller Auto Co., 181 Wis. 72, 193 N.W. 998 (1923); Kahn v. Lesser, 97 Wis. 217, 72 N.W. 739 (1897).

[19] For example, in discussing a statute prohibiting cognovit judgments, the Indiana Court referred to "the evil of having judgments confessed ... on the authority of prematurely executed powers of confession, and without having an opportunity to appear and defend." Peoples Nat'l Bank & Trust Co. v. Pora, 212 Ind. 468, 475, 9 N.E.2d 83, 85 (1937).

[20] WIS. STAT. § 270.69(1) (1967). This limitation is not found in most other states.

[21] 208 Wis. 104, 241 N.W. 337 (1932).

with a mere notation of an amount or amounts payable, but a "promissory note." The common concept of a promissory note is a unilateral instrument containing the express and absolute promise of the signer to pay to a specified person or order, or to bearer, or to a specified person, a definite sum of money at a specified time.[22]

Consequently a promissory note is not a note within the meaning of the statute if it is subject to the terms of an extrinsic contract.[23] However, mere reference to a conditional sales contract does not destroy its character as a note.[24] To qualify for a cognovit proceeding, the note or bond must show on its face that no contingency other than a default in payments will make anything due under the contract.[25] It is apparent that the court is unwilling to hold the cognovit proceeding available to creditors whose own performance in the transaction may give rise to legal defenses.

C. The Debtor's Authorization

Under the Uniform Commercial Code, the authorization clause does not destroy the negotiability of an otherwise negotiable instrument,[26] and the court has held that the assignee of the creditor on a negotiable note may exercise the cognovit provision against the authorizing debtor.[27] But, the court has also held that the cognovit provision may be exercised only against the person who authorized it.[28]

D. The Maturity of the Debt

The language of the statute seems to indicate that judgment may be rendered on a note that is not yet due.[29] However, the court has held that this language must be read in conjunction with *Wisconsin Statutes* section 272.05(7) which states that execution may issue for the collection of those installments which have become due.[30] Thus, the only judgments permitted are those which declare any existing immaturity; execution may issue and be enforced only for the part then due.[31]

E. Outstanding Equities Doctrine

The cognovit proceeding is a special proceeding under *Wisconsin*

---

22 *Id.* at 105, 241 N.W. at 338.
23 Shawano Fin. Corp. v. Julius, 214 Wis. 637, 641, 254 N.W. 355, 357 (1934).
24 Thorp v. Mindeman, 123 Wis. 149, 101 N.W. 417 (1904).
25 United Fin. Corp. v. Peterson, 208 Wis. 104, 106, 241 N.W. 337, 338 (1932).
26 WIS. STAT. § 403.112(d) (1967).
27 Halfhill v. Malick, 145 Wis. 200, 129 N.W. 1086 (1911).
28 Kahn v. Lesser, 97 Wis. 217, 72 N.W. 739 (1897).
29 WIS. STAT. § 270.69(1) (1967).
30 Reeves & Co. v. Kroll, 133 Wis. 196, 113 N.W. 440 (1907).
31 *Id.*

Statutes section 260.03. The equitable nature[32] of the proceeding provides the broadest limitation on the no notice, no day in court objection. Courts of law exercise an equitable jurisdiction over judgments entered by confession and have power, in the exercise of their sound discretion, to open, vacate, or set aside a cognovit judgment upon the showing of good cause.[33] A debtor may move for an order to show cause why the judgment against him should not be set aside. The motion must state facts by affidavit and raise meritorious defenses,[34] which can be equitable[35] or legal.[36] The strong policy in favor of granting a defendant his day in court for an impartial trial[37] has been reflected in the court's holding that it is an abuse of discretion for a judge to refuse to reopen a cognovit judgment upon the defendant's presentation of a proper affidavit.[38]

The ability of the defendant to raise valid objections was enhanced by a 1967 amendment to the cognovit statute, under which the debtor is guaranteed notice of the entry of judgment within thirty days.[39]

F. Summary

It appears that the cognovit proceeding has been well administered in Wisconsin. The criticism that the defendant is not given an opportunity for judicial hearing has been, to some extent, met by the court's strict construction of the statute and by the equitable procedures for reopening judgment.

The harsh cases arise when a negotiable promissory note, which represents the debt arising out of a contract for goods or services, is negotiated to a finance company. A cognovit judgment can then be entered against the debtor in spite of any legal defenses he may have to the underlying transaction. Fundamentally, however, the result is caused by the holder in due course doctrine and not the cognovit procedure.

G. New Developments

Opposition to the cognovit statute remains, however. A recently enacted statute declares the cognovit judgment insufficient for purposes of a garnishment of wages,[40] and current legislative activity

---

32   Kahn v. Lesser, 97 Wis. 217, 72 N.W. 739 (1897).
33   Wessling v. Hieb, 180 Wis. 160, 164, 192 N.W. 458, 459 (1923).
34   Herfurth v. Biederstaedt, 43 Wis. 633 (1878).
35   *See, e.g.,* United Brethren Church v. Vandusen, 37 Wis. 54 (1875) in which the judgment was vacated because of fraud in the underlying transaction.
36   *See, e.g.,* Chippewa Valley Sec. Co. v. Herbst, 227 Wis. 422, 278 N.W. 872 (1938) in which the judgment was vacated because the court lacked jurisdiction.
37   Wessling v. Hieb, 180 Wis. 160, 167, 192 N.W. 458, 460 (1923).
38   Winternitz v. Schmidt, 161 Wis. 421, 154 N.W. 626 (1915).
39   WIS. STAT. § 270.69(3) (1967) created by ch. 36 [1967] Wis. Laws.
40   Ch. 127, § 15 [1969] Wis. Laws —, creating WIS. STAT. § 270.69(4)

in two other areas could determine the future of the cognovit judgment.

The first is a joint resolution which provides for a study of the Uniform Commercial Credit Code for purposes of possible future enactment.[41] Section 2.415 of this model code purports to eliminate confession of judgment by warrant of attorney.[42] The drafters' comment stresses the importance of having a judicial hearing prior to judgment.[43]

The second is a bill which was introduced in September 1969.[44] It calls for an elimination of present cognovit procedure.[45]

II. REGULATION Z

Regulation Z, section 226.9, provides for a right of rescission in any credit transaction in which a security interest may be retained in the customer's principal dwelling.[46]

"Security interest" was not defined in the Truth in Lending Act, but Regulation Z defines it to include "consensual or confessed liens whether or not recorded."[47] The Federal Reserve Board of Governors has on many occasions indicated that confession of judgment clauses will be considered security interests and will give rise to the right of rescission.[48] The reason for this interpretation is that a properly entered judgment becomes a lien on the real property of the judgment debtor, including his principal dwelling. Subject to the $10,000 homestead exemption,[49] this is true in Wisconsin.[50] The right of rescission exists only because of the possibility of this type of lien, and the Board of Governors has conceded that there would be no right of rescission if the terms of the cognovit clause excluded a lien on the principal dwelling.[51] Furthermore, no right of rescission could arise if the consumer did not own a principal dwelling

---

reads as follows: "There shall be no garnishment of earnings based on a judgment without action."

[41] S.J. Res. 54, Wis. Legis. (1969).

[42] The section reads as follows: "A buyer or lessee may not authorize any person to confess judgment on a claim arising out of a consumer credit sale or consumer lease. An authorization in violation of this section is void."

[43] See UNIFORM COMMERCIAL CREDIT CODE § 2.415, Comment.

[44] S. 677, Wis. Legis. (1969).

[45] Section 2 of the Bill reads: "No judgment upon a bond or promissory note shall be rendered, without action, either for money due or to become due."

[46] See note 10, supra, for exceptions.

[47] Reg. Z § 226.2(z).

[48] See note 11, supra.

[49] WIS. STAT. § 272.20 (1967). The first $10,000 of equity in a homestead is exempt from judgment liens in Wisconsin.

[50] WIS. STAT. § 270.79 (1967).

[51] See Truth in Lending Act interpretation letter from M.W. Schober, July 10, 1969, reprinted in 1 CCH CONSUMER CREDIT GUIDE ¶ 3779.

at the time of the credit transaction.[52] In Wisconsin, there would
be no right of rescission if, at the time of the credit transaction, the
consumer had less than $10,000 of equity in his principal dwelling.[53]

The effect of the Truth in Lending Act's right of rescission on
Wisconsin cognovit procedure is dependent upon the specific application of the Federal Reserve Board's definition of security interest.[54] The Board's conclusion that a cognovit clause gives the
holder of an otherwise unsecured note a security interest in the
debtor's principal dwelling can be analyzed on two levels: first
as a legal conclusion, and secondly as a policy judgment.

The notion that a cognovit clause, in itself, creates a security interest at the time of the credit transaction is inconsistent with the
legal effect of such a clause. The traditional concept is that a secured party has a present property interest in the real property
which secures the debt. This interest is insurable;[55] it is taxable;[56]
it may be the basis of a quiet title action against other claimants
to the land; and it allows the secured party to maintain an action
against the debtor for waste or impairment of security.[57] In contrast, the holder of an unsecured note containing a cognovit clause
has no present property interest in the debtor's principal dwelling;
although he does have the possibility of a judgment lien. However,

---

[52] See Truth in Lending Act interpretation letter from J.L. Robertson,
August 15, 1969, reprinted in 1 CCH CONSUMER CREDIT GUIDE ¶ 3806–14.

[53] This conclusion is a consequence of Wisconsin's homestead exemption
statute. Wis. Stat. § 272.20 (1967). In evaluating the effect of the Truth in
Lending Act on cognovit practices in other jurisdictions, one must refer to
the statutory law on homestead exemptions for that jurisdiction.

[54] See note 47, supra. There is no definition of the term in the Truth
in Lending Act, and there is some feeling that Regulation Z has expanded
the right of rescission beyond the intent of Congress.

The argument used by Congressional critics of the Board's broad definition of security interest is based on the legislative history of the Act's
right of rescission provision. Specifically, it is asserted that the Congressional intent was to make the right of rescission apply where non-
purchase-money mortgages were created by the consumer. In other words,
Congress did intend a narrow definition of security interest. For a more
detailed presentation of this argument, see 115 CONG. REC. E5927, E5928
(daily ed. July 15, 1969) (remarks of Mr. Martin).

The argument which the Federal Reserve Board offers in defense of
the broad definition is that if the right of rescission were limited to re-
cordable liens, then creditors could use cognovit provisions to avoid the
right of rescission. In this connection see letter from J.L. Robertson,
March 14, 1969, reprinted in 1 CCH CONSUMER CREDIT GUIDE ¶ 3686.

For the legislative history of the Truth in Lending Act's right of
rescission see 114 CONG. REC. 1610, 1611 (1968) (remarks of Mr. Cahill);
114 CONG. REC. 14384 (1968) (remarks of Mr. Patman); 114 CONG. REC.
14388 (1968) (remarks of Mrs. Sullivan); 114 CONG. REC. 14389 (1968) (remarks of Mr. Cahill).

[55] 36 AM. JUR. Mortgages § 324 (1941).

[56] 36 AM. JUR. Mortgages § 350 (1941).

[57] 36 AM. JUR. Mortgages § 316 (1941). See also Dick & Reuteman Co.
v. Jem Realty Co., 225 Wis. 428, 274 N.W. 416 (1937).

at the time of the credit transaction, it is speculative to assert that the creditor will ever have such an interest. In Wisconsin this interest is contingent on three things: (1) that the debtor will default; (2) that the court will enter a cognovit judgment; and (3) that the debtor will have $10,000 of equity in his principal dwelling.

Therefore, in defining and interpreting the term "security interest," the Federal Reserve Board did not apply existing law. The idea that a cognovit clause creates a security interest was born with the issuance and interpretation of Regulation Z.

The broad definition of "security interest" was, it seems, a policy decision. Perhaps the Federal Reserve Board wanted to protect consumers by providing a right of rescission against hard sell-quick exit sellers. Since it is a fair assumption that most unscrupulous seller-creditors use cognovit clauses, the Board superficially accomplished the protection by defining "security interest" to include cognovit clauses.

There are at least two serious problems with this logic. First, those consumers who need protection the most will not get it. Generally, the poor and unsophisticated consumers are those most in need of the right of rescission. Since they are not likely to have $10,000 of equity in their principal dwelling, they will be denied the right of rescission.

Secondly, the unscrupulous sellers will simply stop using cognovit clauses. The cognovit judgment was never crucial to their operation because, in the vast majority of cases, the fly-by-night seller was not concerned with collection. He promptly negotiated the buyer's obligation to a finance company which took the note as a holder in due course. In the absence of a cognovit clause, finance companies and sellers who handle their own collections will obtain judgment against defaulting buyers through ordinary civil actions. This may further disadvantage the buyer since he may be taxed with higher court costs than if the judgment had been on cognovit.

The most likely explanation for the broad definition of "security interest" is that the Federal Reserve Board wanted to wage a direct attack on cognovit judgments in the consumer area. The problem here is the haphazard fashion in which it was done. Congress could have prohibited cognovit judgments as a part of the Truth in Lending Act; it did not.[58] But by putting the label of security interest on cognovit provisions, the Federal Reserve Board has effectively discouraged their use. Creditors have discontinued using cognovit clauses principally because Regulation Z forces them to withhold their performance in a transaction until they are satis-

[58] The original House Bill did have a provision prohibiting cognovit judgments. The compromise Senate Bill which was enacted deleted that provision.

fied that the customer will not rescind.[59]

The objection to cognovit judgments is that defendants are not given the opportunity for a judicial hearing before the judgment is granted. The Wisconsin court has mitigated this objectionable feature by a careful administration of cognovit procedure. Cognovit procedure in Wisconsin does not deny a defendant the opportunity to raise defenses; it merely alters the time at which they can be raised. Whatever objections remain are partially balanced by the efficiency and low cost of the cognovit proceeding as opposed to a civil action. But it seems that the Federal Reserve Board did not consider these circumstances in reaching its conclusion.[60]

In conclusion, the Federal Reserve Board's attack on cognovit judgments was, in terms of Wisconsin law, a misguided attack on the wrong evil. By administrative fiat, it did what neither Congress nor the Wisconsin legislature has thus far been willing to do. This is not objectionable, but one fears that it was done for the wrong reasons. The Truth in Lending Act's right of rescission is largely an attack on unscrupulous sellers. In Wisconsin the attempt to reach these sellers by making the right of rescission apply whenever cognovit provisions are used will fail because unscrupulous sellers will simply stop using cognovit provisions. The result is an attack on cognovit procedure irrespective of its merits as an economical and efficient judicial proceeding.

Perhaps Congress will amend the right of rescission provision in the Truth in Lending Act. Perhaps some lender will challenge, via declaratory judgment, the authority of the Federal Reserve Board to define security interests as including cognovit provisions. Absent these events, Wisconsin cognovit procedure will either fall entirely into disuse in consumer transactions, or it will be used selectively on those consumers who have less than $10,000 of equity in their principal dwelling.

---

[59] Reg. Z § 226.9(c).

[60] Of course, one cannot expect the Federal Reserve Board to be especially sensitive to the law of any one state. The cognovit judgment is a creature of state law, and, as such, its administration varies greatly among different jurisdictions. Many states prohibit cognovit judgments. Others administer cognovit procedure quite differently than does Wisconsin. Therefore, in evaluating the Federal Reserve Board's definition of security interest, one must look closely to state law. For an overview of each state's treatment of cognovit procedure, see 1 CCH CONSUMER CREDIT GUIDE ¶ 610. *See also* 2 CCH CONSUMER CREDIT GUIDE.

Conspiracy
Historical Perspectives

An Arno Press Collection

CATILINE AND THE ROMAN CONSPIRACY: Two Accounts, 1721-1910. 1972.

CONSPIRACY OF ARNOLD, AND SIR HENRY CLINTON, AGAINST THE UNITED STATES, AND AGAINST GENERAL WASHINGTON. (Reprinted from *The American Register*, Volume II, 1817.)

THE CONSPIRACY TRIAL FOR THE MURDER OF THE PRESIDENT. Edited with an Introduction, by Ben: Perley Poore. Three volumes. 1865/1866.

Hutchinson, Lester.
CONSPIRACY AT MEERUT. 1935.

Knox, J. Wendell.
CONSPIRACY IN AMERICAN POLITICS, 1787-1815. 1964.

LEGAL CONCEPTS OF CONSPIRACY: A Law Review Trilogy, 1922-1970. 1972.

Wilkinson, George Theodore.
AN AUTHENTIC HISTORY OF THE CATO-STREET CONSPIRACY. [1820].

Related Books

Bew, J., publisher
MINUTES OF A CONSPIRACY AGAINST THE LIBERTIES OF AMERICA. 1865.

Blankenhorn, Heber
THE STRIKE FOR UNION. 1924.

Brackenridge, Henry M.
HISTORY OF THE WESTERN INSURRECTION IN WESTERN PENNSYLVANIA, COMMONLY CALLED THE WHISKEY INSURRECTION, 1794. 1859.

Burns, William J.
THE MASKED WAR: The Story of a Peril That Threatened the United States by the Man Who Uncovered the Dynamite Conspirators and Sent Them to Jail. 1913.

Calkins, Clinch
SPY OVERHEAD: The Story of Industrial Espionage. 1937.

Carroll, Charles
JOURNAL OF CHARLES CARROLL OF CARROLLTON, During
His Visit to Canada in 1776, as One of the Commissioners From
Congress; With a Memoir and Notes by Brantz Mayor. 1876.

Clark, Daniel
PROOFS OF THE CORRUPTION OF GEN. JAMES WILKINSON,
and of His Connexion With Aaron Burr, With a Full Refutation of
His Slanderous Allegations in Relation to the Character of the
Principal Witness Against Him. 1809.

Coleman, J. Walter
THE MOLLY MAGUIRE RIOTS: Industrial Conflict in the
Pennsylvania Coal Region. 1936.

Dacus, Joseph A.
ANNALS OF THE GREAT STRIKES. 1877.

Davis, William Watts Hart
THE FRIES REBELLION: 1798-1799; An Armed Resistance to the
House Tax Law Passed by Congress, July 9, 1798 in Bucks and
Northampton Counties, Pennsylvania. 1899.

Dawson, Henry B.
THE SONS OF LIBERTY IN NEW YORK. 1859.

A GENUINE NARRATIVE OF THE INTENDED CONSPIRACY
OF THE NEGROES AT ANTIGUA. 1737.

George, Harrison
THE I.W.W. TRIAL: The Story of the Greatest Trial in Labor's
History by One of the Defendants.

Hiller, Ernest T.
THE STRIKE: A Study in Collective Action. 1928.

Hillquit, Morris, Samuel Gompers, and Max J. Hayes
THE DOUBLE EDGE OF LABOR'S SWORD: Discussion and
Testimony on Socialism and Trade-Unionism Before the Commission
on Industrial Relations. 1914.

Hough, Emerson
THE WEB. 1919.

House of Representatives
THE KU KLUX KLAN: 67th Congress, 1st Session, House Committee
on Rules Hearings. 1921.

Kampelman, Max M.
THE COMMUNIST PARTY vs. THE C.I.O.: A Study in Power
Politics. 1957.

Lane, Winthrop D.
CIVIL WAR IN WEST VIRGINIA. 1921.

Langdon, Emma F.
THE CRIPPLE CREEK STRIKE: A History of Industrial Wars in
   Colorado 1903-4-5; Being a Complete and Concise History of the
   Efforts of Organized Capital to Crush Unionism. 1905.

Levinson, Edward
I BREAK STRIKES! The Technique of Pearl L. Bergoff. 1935.

Lum, Dyer D.
A CONCISE HISTORY OF THE GREAT TRIAL OF THE
   CHICAGO ANARCHISTS IN 1886: Condensed from the Official
   Record. n.d.

Manhattan, Avro
CATHOLIC IMPERIALISM AND WORLD FREEDOM. 1952.

Mason, Alpheus T.
ORGANIZED LABOR AND THE LAW. 1925.

Parsons, Lucy, editor
THE FAMOUS SPEECHES OF THE EIGHT CHICAGO
   ANARCHISTS IN COURT. 1910.

Pinkerton, Allan
STRIKES, COMMUNISTS, TRAMPS AND DETECTIVES. 1878.

Safford, William H.
THE BLENNERHASSETT PAPERS. 1864.

Select Committee of the Senate
THE INVASION AT HARPER'S FERRY: 36th Congress, 1st
   Session, Senate Report No. 278. 1860.

Smith, Joshua Hett
AN AUTHENTIC NARRATIVE OF THE DEATH OF MAJOR
   ANDRE. 1808.

Socialist Publishing Society
THE ACCUSED AND THE ACCUSERS. 1887.

Special Committee of the Senate to Investigate Organized Crime in
Interstate Commerce
REPORTS ON CRIME INVESTIGATIONS: 82nd Congress, 1st
   Session, Senate Reports. 1951.

Stein, Leon and Philip Taft, editors
THE PULLMAN STRIKE. 1894-1913

Tallmadge, Benjamin
MEMOIR OF COLONEL BENJAMIN TALLMADGE, PREPARED
   BY HIMSELF AT THE REQUEST OF HIS CHILDREN. 1858.

Victor, Orville J.
HISTORY OF THE AMERICAN CONSPIRACIES: A Record of Treason, Insurrection, Rebellion, etc. in the United States of America, from 1760 to 1860. 1863.

Wells, H. G.
CRUX ANSATA: An Indictment of the Roman Catholic Church. 1944.

Witte, Edwin Emil
THE GOVERNMENT IN LABOR DISPUTES. 1932.

Wolman, Leo
THE BOYCOTT IN AMERICAN TRADE UNIONS. 1916.